Midwest Living®

MISSISSIPPI RIVER GETAWAYS

ALL NEW

Meredith® Books
Des Moines, Iowa

The imperious Mississippi River clefts the country in two, defining the borders of 10 states as it flows—sometimes broad and shallow, sometimes deep and narrow—an astonishing 2,348 miles from Minnesota to Louisiana. Long before Europeans arrived, the Algonquin Indians recognized the river's might and gave it an appropriately majestic name: Mississippi, "Father of Waters."

The meandering river was the Heartland's 19th-century highway, carrying lumber and lead, adventurers and entrepreneurs. Fleets of paddle wheelers and steamboats plied the waters, bringing dry goods, mail and passengers to the towns that flourished along the Mississippi's banks and high atop its limestone bluffs.

There's an irresistible and timeless romance to the Mississippi River, captured in the writings of Mark Twain. His much-loved tales of Tom Sawyer and Huck Finn were affectionate remembrances of his own boyhood adventures in the river town of Hannibal, Missouri. Years later, Twain took a sentimental journey down the river and wrote about it in *Life on the Mississippi*. Read it and before you know it, you're itching to see the big river for yourself.

Mississippi River Getaways will help you do that. We follow the Mississippi through the Midwest, highlighting 16 can't-miss destinations, from the river's crystalline beginnings as a narrow stream in Minnesota's north woods to the cypress swamps of southern Illinois. You can choose a big-city weekend with sophisticated options for dining and nightlife or opt for a small-town stopover, where you can cap a day of antiquing with a catfish dinner.

In each chapter, we'll take a few pages to give you a detailed account about a town or two, then move on to a travel guide that lists places to stay and to eat, annual events, nearby attractions and phone numbers to call for more information. Each region includes a basic map and full-color photos that preview some of the people and places that make these Midwest destinations special.

Lake Itasca

MINNESOTA

MICHIGAN

●Brainerd

Mississippi River

St. Cloud●

Minneapolis/St. Paul●

WISCONSIN

Redwing● ●Stockholm
●Alma
Winona● ●Trempealeau
●La Crosse

McGregor● ●Prairie du Chien
Guttenberg●
Dubuque● ●Galena

IOWA

Mississippi River

Quad Cities●

NEBRASKA

Keokuk● ●Nauvoo

●Quincy
Hannibal●

ILLINOIS

Elsah● ●Alton
St. Louis●

MISSOURI

Mississippi River

KANSAS

Ste. Genevieve●

Cape Girardeau●
Cairo●
KENTUCKY

OKLAHOMA

ARKANSAS   Caruthersville●
TENNESSEE

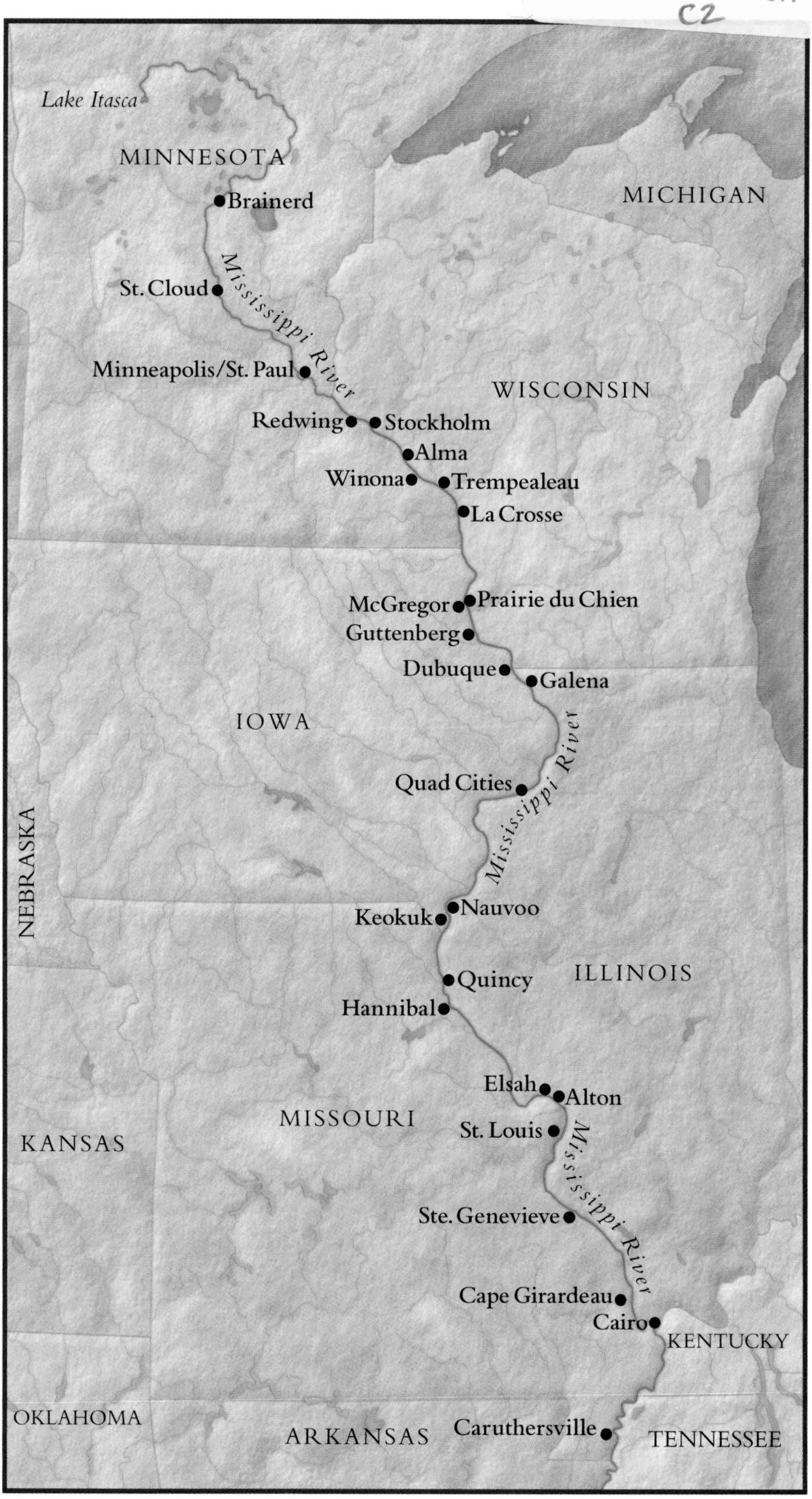

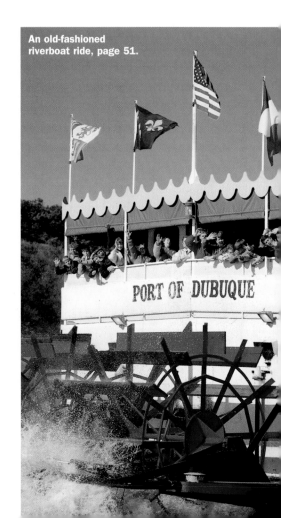

Hikers near Wabasha, page 30.

Adirondack Coffee House,
page 14.

An old-fashioned
riverboat ride, page 51.

PORT OF DUBUQUE

CONTENTS

Shawnee National Forest, page 134.

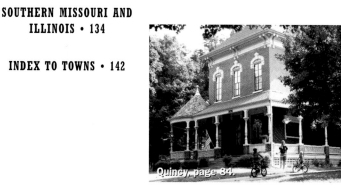

Quincy, page 84.

NORTHERN WATERS

The Mississippi River takes its tentative first steps in Minnesota's lake country, a toddler of a stream, leaving Lake Itasca with little indication of the powerful, handsome waterway it becomes as it flows toward the Gulf of Mexico. Curving through forests, the river gathers strength from countless streams.

Lumberjacks reminiscent of mythical Paul Bunyan stripped away much of Minnesota's virgin timber. However, you still can see towering old-growth red and white pine in Itasca State Park, the 32,000-acre sanctuary that preserves the ancient trees and protects the headwaters area.

Heading south and east, the Mississippi reaches Minneapolis and St. Paul, cities that grew up on opposite sides of the river. Although different in character, both are charming, cultured and thoroughly enjoyable—filled with theaters, museums, restaurants, historic districts and shops.

South of the Twin Cities, the Mississippi's massive limestone bluffs become more pronounced. At Red Wing, you'll get the flavor of what many prosperous river towns were like in the 19th century. Flanked by the towering bluffs and the river, rows of well-tended red brick storefronts line downtown streets.

Downstream from Red Wing, the Mississippi River lingers to form Lake Pepin. Three miles wide and 22 miles long, the waters lap at the shores of bluff-side towns where sailboats bob in almost every harbor and the coffeepot always brews at the corner cafe.

Once past the Chippewa River, the Mississippi narrows again. On the Minnesota side, Wabasha and Winona beckon,

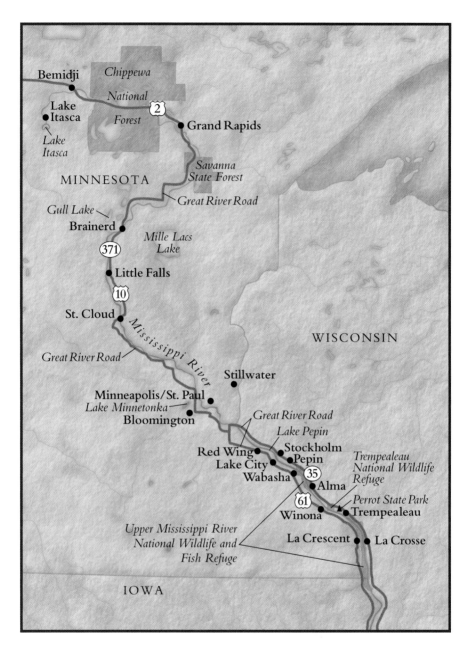

with venerable architecture and bluff-top parks for grand
river views. Follow the Great River Road along the
Wisconsin shore to Trempealeau, where you can watch
barge traffic ease through Lock and Dam No. 6. Toward
evening, stake out a spot on the deck at the Trempealeau
Hotel and watch the sun set on another fine day along
the Mississippi River.

MISSISSIPPI HEADWATERS

In a land of towering trees and a burly fellow named Paul Bunyan, a great river begins its journey.

The cool, clear stream slipping out of central Minnesota's Lake Itasca tickles your ankles as you take a dozen quick steps to the opposite bank. The narrow pathway of water glides over pebbles and pushes past boulders, its whisper mingling with the wind murmuring through virgin pine forest. This is the Mississippi River, starting out modestly on a grand 2,348-mile journey to the Gulf of Mexico.

Here, in headwaters country, the river wends its way between banks of waist-high grass and meanders through lakes before curving south, gaining strength as it goes. By the time the Mississippi River reaches St. Cloud 54 miles northwest of Minneapolis, it flows wide and deep.

Paul Bunyan Country

In this part of Minnesota, the Mississippi is just one giant in a land of giants. Trees stand cathedral-tall, lakes stretch their shorelines out for miles, and the legendary lumberjack, Paul Bunyan, looms large in collective memory. Science teaches that the area's 1,000-plus lakes formed when Ice Age glaciers gouged the land, then melted. But it's much more fun to picture Bunyan's enormous blue ox, Babe, prancing across the countryside, leaving giant hoofprints that later filled with water.

Bunyan symbolizes the brawny logging industry that brought prosperity to the towns along this part of the Mississippi in the mid-1800s. Though many forests were left bleak and barren in logging's aftermath, conservation efforts have rejuvenated the thick woodlands. Now, countless lakeside lodges and fishing camps draw visitors to a region teeming with fish, fowl and friendly folks.

Geologist and Indian agent Henry Schoolcraft is credited with tracing the Mississippi's origins in 1832 to the lake he named Itasca. In 1891, the state set aside 32,000 acres of virgin pine forests surrounding the hallowed headwaters as Lake Itasca State Park, one of the first state parks in the country. That move stopped encroachment by the lumber companies, leaving the park with one of the few remaining stands of the ancient, skyscraper-high evergreens in the U.S.

Canoeing the
Mississippi River
near Lake
Winnibigoshish.

From Bemidji to Brainerd

Bemidji calls itself the "First City on the Mississippi." The river glides through the bustling town (population: 11,509), horseshoeing around the foot of Lake Bemidji. Dozens of motels and resorts cater to the hikers and bikers who explore the tree-lined shore and anglers who troll the lake for walleye, northern pike, muskie, perch, crappie, panfish and largemouth bass.

A statue of Bunyan himself, resembling a mustachioed Frenchman wearing a plaid flannel shirt, stands 18 feet tall beside his blue ox Babe, next to the Bemidji Tourist Information Center. Erected in 1937, these figures "pose" for countless pictures.

The Mississippi sidles out of Lake Bemidji's eastern shore and winds its way east through the big lakes of Cass and Winnibigoshish, "Lake Winnie" to locals. In fall, birches, maples, oaks and elms curtain the two lakes, splashing bright yellows, oranges and reds on the evergreen canvas of pines and tamaracks.

Follow State-46 through the center of the Chippewa National Forest between Northome and Deer River, and you'll end up on the 39-mile Avenue of Pines. Norway pines line the highway, standing at attention like colossal soldiers on review.

At Grand Rapids (population: 7,976) the Mississippi turns south. In the latter half of the 19th century, steamboats chugged upriver from Minneapolis and St. Paul, 175 miles to the south, bringing supplies to the logging boomtown. Grand Rapids celebrates its lumber heyday at the Forest History Center, where costumed interpreters reenact life in a 1900 lumberjack camp.

Before continuing south on the National Great River Road (County-3), follow the yellow brick road to the Old Central School, now a museum with memorabilia of Grand Rapids' favorite daughter, Judy Garland.

After twisting and turning through Savanna State Forest, the Mississippi flows into Brainerd, 134 miles northwest of the Twin Cities. The town is the geographic center of the state and the self-proclaimed hometown of Bunyan. His silo-size likeness—and another tall structure, a yellow, torch-shaped water tower—greets visitors to this town of 12,353, surrounded by 465 sandy-shored lakes. Minnesota's first lakeside lodges appeared here in the late 19th

Cragun's Lodge hugs Gull Lake's shoreline near Brainerd.

LAYNE KENNEDY

In Crosby, Hallett House, a 1920s inn.

century, and many still thrive as plush resorts run by the third and fourth generations of founding families. Some of the oldest and most popular lodges look out on the 86-mile shoreline of Mille Lacs (French for "1,000 lakes"), Minnesota's largest lake. The lake nourishes more than 40 species of fish, loons, and migrating ducks and geese.

The River Dips and Stretches

Thirty miles downstream, at an 11-foot drop in the Mississippi, settlers founded the aptly named town of Little Falls (population: 1,100). On a woodsy rise near the falls, a modest, gray-washed bungalow watches the river go by. U.S. Congressman Charles A. Lindbergh, Sr., built the Craftsman-style house as a summer retreat in 1906. His son Charles, Jr., lived there and managed the farm through high school, then flew into aviation history in *The Spirit of St. Louis*.

At St. Cloud, the Mississippi widens and straightens, cutting through land rich with fertile soil above and granite below. German Catholics settled in large numbers here, and the city (population: 48,812) reflects the founding fathers' religious devotion in its centuries-old churches and secluded college campuses. Orchestra, choral group and theater productions fill cultural calendars throughout the year. Stroll the brick walkways of the Munsinger and Clemens Gardens downtown on the banks of the Mississippi. Breathe deeply as summer breezes coax the fragrance from roses, red salvia, hostas, mums, irises, daffodils and wax begonias.

The Mississippi that began in Lake Itasca as a stream leaves St. Cloud a full-blown river. As folklore recounts, Paul Bunyan created this phenomenon when a tank wagon hauled by Babe sprang a leak. The water rushed all the way to Mexico.

Born where the trees grow tall and the lakes number a thousand, this river was destined to be mighty.

TRAVEL GUIDE

Planning Your Visit to the Headwaters

For more information about north-central Minnesota, contact: Minnesota Office of Tourism (800/657-3700).

Lake Itasca

Contact: Lake Itasca State Park (218/266-2114; 218/266-2100).

LODGINGS

Douglas Lodge—Stay in the renovated 1903 log lodge or neighboring motel and cabins. The lodge has two full-service restaurants. Doubles from $44 (800/246-2267).

SIGHTSEEING

Lake Itasca—Board the 55-passenger *Chester Charles* for naturalist-narrated tours around the lake (218/732-5318). The 32,000-acre Itasca State Park, 223 miles northwest of the Twin Cities, offers camping, swimming, boating, fishing, hiking and biking. In winter, the paths turn into snowmobiling, snowshoeing and cross-country ski trails (218/266-2100).

Bemidji

Contact: Bemidji Area Visitors & Convention Bureau (800/458-2223).

LODGINGS

Finn 'n' Feather Resort—Three generations of owners welcome guests to 19 log and wood-paneled homes overlooking Lake Andrusia, 10 miles east of Bemidji. Weekly rates from $890 (800/776-3466).

Lakewatch Bed & Breakfast—This comfortable 1904 house, with four guest rooms and private baths, is in a neighborhood of historic homes along Lake Blvd. Doubles from $40 (218/751-8413).

A Place in the Woods—Secluded, handsomely furnished log cabins offer a quiet haven. Doubles from $130 (800/676-4547).

Ruttger's Birchmont Lodge—Lakeside lodge rooms, deluxe cottages and modern townhomes form a full-service resort. Doubles from $78 (888/RUTTGER).

DINING

Chocolates Plus—Treat yourself to hand-dipped candies and specialty coffees (218/759-1175).

Union Station—The old train depot has been restored as a restaurant (218/751-9261).

SHOPPING

Bemidji Woolen Mills—Find red-and-black-checked woolen shirts and other north-woods wear (218/751-5166).

Emily's Country Cottage—Expect a singular collection of handmade gifts and collectibles (218/751-6387).

Gallery North—Local artists display paintings, prints and artwork (218/759-9813).

The Old Schoolhouse—More than 500 artists display paintings and crafts (218/751-4723).

Snow Goose Gifts—Look for loons, ladyslippers, wind chimes and other Minnesota-made items (218/751-5522).

ATTRACTIONS

Lake Bemidji State Park—Head for the lake's north shore for camping, swimming, hiking and a boardwalk stroll over a bog (218/755-3843).

Paul Bunyan Playhouse—Minnesota's oldest summer theater presents musicals and plays (218/751-7270).

WINTER ACTIVITIES

Buena Vista Ski Area—One of Minnesota's oldest downhill slopes north of Bemidji offers snowboarding and cross-country skiing (218/243-2231).

Cross-country skiing—Nordic skiers choose between the 4k Montebello Trail downtown and the Movil Maze, a hilly course favored by experts (800/458-2223).

Brrrmidji Polar Daze—During the third week

of January, the town hosts snowmobile runs, sleigh rides, snow sculpting and concerts (800/458-2223).

Logging Days—Each February, lumberjacks show off their skills with snaggletoothed saws, while visitors eat flap-jacks and ride sleighs at the Buena Vista Ski Area north of Bemidji (218/243-2231).

villas with whirlpools. Doubles from $78 (800/450-4555).

DINING

The First Grade Restaurant—This eatery in the Old Central School is famed for turkey and all the trimmings (218/326-9361).

Forest Lake Restaurant— Stop here for sizzling steaks (218/326-3423).

area history (218/327-4482).

Old Central School—The restored school houses a restaurant, gift shops and the Itasca Heritage Center, with exhibits about Judy Garland (218/327-1843).

FESTIVALS

Judy Garland Festival— There's no place like home. For Judy Garland, that would be Grand Rapids, which celebrates her career in June (800/664-JUDY).

Mississippi Melodie Showboat—A cast of 70 brings 1800s vaudeville and dance to life in July (800/722-7814).

Tall Timber Days— This August celebration includes lumberjack shows, an arts-and-crafts fair, canoe and turtle races, 5k and 10k runs, a parade and chainsaw carving (800/GRAND MN).

GREG RYAN

Matthew Fossen rides a Scottish Highland bull during Buena Vista Ski Area Logging Days Festival.

Grand Rapids

Contact: Grand Rapids Chamber of Commerce (800/472-6366).

LODGINGS

Ruttger's Sugar Lake Lodge—This 400-acre retreat along the forested shore of Sugar Lake, 14 miles south-west of Grand Rapids, has condominiums in the woods and lakeside

ACTIVITIES

Canoeing—Float on the Mississippi in the headwaters region, where the river is suitable for all skill levels. Contact the Chamber of Commerce for area outfitters (800/472-6366).

Forest History Center— Interpreters in this reconstructed 1900 logging camp explain

WINTER ACTIVITIES

Dogsledding—Take a ride behind a team of huskies at Ruttger's Sugar Lake Lodge (800/450-4555).

Brainerd

Contact: Brainerd Lakes Area Chamber of Commerce (800/450-2838, ext. 491).

LODGINGS

Brainerd, with national motel chains in town, is surrounded by resorts,

TRAVEL GUIDE

most offering golf and/or fishing packages. A few choices include:

Breezy Point Resort—This full-service resort north of Brainerd was the honeymoon retreat of Clark Gable and Carole Lombard. Doubles from $109 (800/432-3777).

Cragun's Resort—Suites, cottages and an indoor sports center are part of this 50-year-old resort along Gull Lake. Doubles from $120 (800/CRAGUNS).

Hallett House—This Georgian Revival-style mansion is an elegant bed and breakfast in Crosby, 15 miles northeast of Brainerd. Doubles from $55 (218/546-5433).

Hay Lake Lodge—These townhomes near Pequot Lakes are located 19 miles north of Brainerd. Doubles from $80 (800/HAY-LAKE).

McQuoid's Inn—This resort borders on the southeast shore of Mille Lacs. Doubles from $60 (218/862-3535).

Quarterdeck Resort & Restaurant—Gull Lake laps the shore near this resort in Nisswa, 17 miles northwest of Brainerd. Doubles from $106 (800/950-5596).

DINING

Adirondack Coffee House—Savor fresh soup and bread in a restored hotel in Nisswa, 13 miles

north of Brainerd (218/963-3421).

Iven's on the Bay—This lakeside eatery specializes in fresh lake fish and homemade desserts (218/829-9872).

Last Turn Saloon—A historic pub, it serves Minnesota wild-rice soup and sandwiches (218/829-4856).

SHOPPING

Kinzie Candles—This shop in Pequot Lakes stocks candles made in antique glassware molds (218/568-8828).

Silver Creek Traders—Discover handmade furniture in Pequot Lakes (218/568-5144).

Woodland Meadow—Look for whimsical hand-crafted birdhouses and folk art in Nisswa, 13 miles north of Brainerd (218/963-0036).

ACTIVITIES

Golf—Dense woods and wilderness vistas have helped turn Brainerd into a golf mecca. More than 24 courses lie between Pequot Lake, 19 miles north of Brainerd, and Mille Lacs, 17 miles east. Two new layouts: The Preserve at Grand View Lodge near Nisswa (800/432-3788) and The Classic at Madden's on Gull Lake (800/642-5363). Contact: Brainerd Lakes Area Chamber of Commerce (800/450-2838, ext. 491).

ATTRACTIONS

Paul Bunyan Amusement Center—Enjoy rides, logging exhibits and a 26-foot animated statue of Paul Bunyan and Babe (218/829-6342).

WINTER ACTIVITIES

Northland Arboretum—This area covers 20 kilometers of groomed and tracked Nordic trails (800/450-2838).

Ski Gull—This downhill ski area north of town with 14 runs focuses on family skiing and children's lessons (218/963-4353).

Expect hearty fare and a north-woods atmosphere at the Adirondack Coffee House in Nisswa.

Little Falls

Contact: Little Falls Chamber of Commerce (800/325-5916).

ATTRACTIONS

Charles A. Lindbergh House—See the boyhood summer home of the aviation pioneer with museum exhibits about the Lindbergh family (320/632-3154).

Pine Grove Park—View a stand of virgin pine (320/632-2341).

FESTIVALS

Arts-and-Crafts Fair—On the weekend after Labor Day, one of the Midwest's largest arts-and-crafts fairs exhibits works of 1,000 crafters (320/632-5155).

St. Cloud

Contact: St. Cloud Area Convention & Visitors Bureau (800/264-2940).

LODGINGS

St. Cloud has chain motels and hotels, and bed and breakfasts. Edelbrock House Bed and Breakfast—This yellow-brick 1880 farmhouse with four guest rooms exudes country charm in the center of the city. Doubles from $60 (320/259-0071). Victorian Oaks—This 1891 home near downtown has three guest rooms. Doubles from $75 (800/476-5035).

DINING

Cyber Bean—Surf the Internet while enjoying soup, homemade desserts and specialty coffees at this east-side hangout (320/252-3332). D.B. Searle's—Enjoy French onion soup and stuffed popovers in a restored 1886 building downtown

(320/253-0655). Pirate's Cove—Try a juicy steak or fresh seafood on the patio overlooking the Mississippi River (320/252-8400).

SHOPPING

Arts Co-Op—Browse among folk art, pottery, needlework, paintings and carvings (320/252-3242). Dolls from the Heart—Collect dolls and bears from Zook, Götz, Himstedt and Gund (320/656-0613).

ACTIVITIES

Biking—Cycle through downtown parks, along the Mississippi River and on backwoods treks. Contact: St. Cloud Convention & Visitors Bureau (800/264-2940). Tubing—At Two Rivers Park, 18 miles north of St. Cloud, tube on the Platte River above its confluence with the Mississippi (320/584-5125).

ATTRACTIONS

Munsinger and Clemens Gardens—Take in flower beds laid out along the banks of the Mississippi River (320/255-7206). Stearns County Heritage Center—Displays feature a replica of a working granite quarry (320/253-8424).

AREA RECREATION & SCENIC DRIVES

North Country National Scenic Trail—Bike 68 miles in Chippewa National Forest, through hills, bogs, grasslands and woods (800/833-1118). Paul Bunyan Trail—Bike or hike 100 miles from Brainerd to Bemidji on an old railroad bed that shadows State-371. In winter, cross-country ski or snowmobile. Contact: Brainerd Lakes Area Chamber of Commerce (800/450-2838, ext. 491) or Bemidji Area Visitors & Convention Bureau (800/458-2223). Chippewa National Forest—Three routes give travelers the best forest scenery: State-46 from Northome to Deer River, 11 miles north-west of Grand Rapids, known as the Avenue of Pines, 39 miles; State-38 north from Grand Rapids to Effie, called the Edge of the Wilderness, 47 miles; County-39 from Blackduck, 25 miles northeast of Bemidji, south to US-2 east of Cass Lake, 28 miles. Mille Lacs Lake—A 52-mile drive circles the lake, a favorite in the fall. Follow State-18 along the north shore, State-47 down the east side, State-27 around the south to US-169 back up the west shoreline.

By Eric Minton

MINNEAPOLIS AND ST. PAUL

The Twin Cities' diverse personalities make vacationing here doubly delightful.

Twins they may be, but these cities are decidedly different. St. Paul is the quiet sibling; Minneapolis shows off for company. St. Paul has been called the "last city of the East," tidily platted and sturdily built by the German and Irish immigrants who settled it. Minneapolis is the "first city of the West," brash and forward-looking, its tall buildings stretching to the sky and the future. Their shared bounty of restaurants, theaters, museums, shopping and sports venues makes one thing certain: In this friendly rivalry, visitors always win.

St. Paul

In 1840, you would have found your way to St. Paul by asking for directions to Pig's Eye Landing. A few crude cabins inhabited by French-Canadian fur traders, farmers and whiskey dealers flanked the rowdy riverside saloon run by Pierre "Pig's Eye" Parrant that gave the settlement its name. Civilization arrived shortly afterward in the form of a log chapel dedicated to St. Paul, and the less-colorful name won out.

Today, the golden, striated river bluffs of downtown St. Paul overlook an expansive view of barge and train traffic along the Mississippi River. Art Deco buildings and Victorian gems of stone and red brick grace streets punctuated by church spires and intimate city parks.

Spend the day exploring St. Paul's dynamic trio of downtown museums: the Minnesota History Center, Science Museum of Minnesota and Minnesota Children's Museum. In the evening, head to Rice Park. This lovely small square acts as an elegant front yard for the sparkling Ordway Music Theatre. Its stage showcases internationally acclaimed local performing groups, such as the St. Paul Chamber Orchestra, as well as touring companies. Across the park, the Art Deco-era St. Paul Hotel lends a cosmopolitan note.

North of downtown, the white dome of the Minnesota State Capitol rises majestically. A boulevard connects this grand 1905 statehouse with the equally imposing domed presence of the Cathedral of St. Paul. Fashioned after St. Peter's in Rome, the commanding hilltop edifice dominates the western skyline.

Historic Summit Avenue, St. Paul's 4½-mile showcase of Victorian residences, runs from the

MICHAEL DOUGLAS

St. Paul's Ordway
Music Theatre
gleams
downtown.

cathedral to the river. Along the stately boulevard stand the craggy, red sandstone mansion of railroad baron James J. Hill and the more modest home of author F. Scott Fitzgerald.

One block south is lively Grand Avenue, with an intriguing array of restaurants and cottage-size shops where potted urns and window boxes display floral panache. A walk down neighboring tree-lined streets reveals cozy homes, friendly porches, vintage lampposts and old-fashioned lilac bushes and peony blooms.

On Saturday evenings, Garrison Keillor drives in from mythical Lake Wobegon to broadcast *A Prairie Home Companion* from St. Paul's prized Fitzgerald Theater.

Minneapolis

Across the river, downtown Minneapolis' glassy skyscrapers sparkle by day and illuminate the night sky.

Minneapolis was born at the site of the Mississippi's only true waterfall, a 16-foot rush that French explorer Father Louis Hennepin named for his patron, St. Anthony. The falls' power, harnessed in the 1820s, produced the area's first sawmill and flour mill, and guaranteed the success of the little village of St. Anthony. Renamed Minneapolis, it was the flour-milling capital of the nation by the 1880s. Follow the Heritage Trail markers to explore the cobblestone streets and wooded pathways of this earliest Minneapolis neighborhood. After dark, music enlivens Southeast Main Street's restaurants and bars, which look west to the downtown skyline along the Mississippi.

Downtown, Nicollet Mall, a pedestrian avenue with fountains, sculptures and inviting cafes, is the premier place for big-name shopping. Neiman Marcus and Saks Fifth Avenue are steps from hometown favorite Dayton's giant multi-level flagship store.

The adjacent Warehouse District is filled with boutiques, galleries and

Minneapolis' Whitney Hotel.

SUSAN GILMORE

Como Park's conservatory.

SUSAN GILMORE

restaurants. Nearby, Hennepin Avenue attracts nighttime crowds to its theater scene. The contemporary, Tony award-winning Guthrie Theater may be the Twin Cities' best-known playhouse, but dozens more, large and small, also claim loyal audiences.

A few minutes' drive southwest from downtown is Uptown. It's an animated community where counterculturalists and conservatives co-exist in a neighborhood of lovely old homes, imaginative restaurants, engaging shops and art-film theaters.

More Metro Area Fun

The southern suburb of Bloomington is home to the Paul Bunyan of shopping centers, the Mall of America. Visitors from as far away as Japan come to marvel at its 400 specialty shops, four anchor stores and a mammoth entertainment complex that includes nightclubs, restaurants and a full-fledged indoor amusement park, complete with a roller coaster. (An extra incentive for shoppers:

There is no sales tax on clothing.)

Lakes and parks link the Twin Cities. Visitors quickly discover that green spaces and blue water are often just around the corner from rush hour traffic. You can rent a canoe at Lake Calhoun for a tranquil paddle through a chain of four lakes bordered by attractive homes. Or bike the Grand Rounds Scenic Byway that encircles Minneapolis with paths filled by walkers, joggers, in-line skaters and cyclists. The 55-mile course passes placid urban lakes, rushing streams and the densely forested Mississippi River Gorge.

St. Paul's first-rate park system includes popular Como Park with its free zoo and Victorian conservatory where flowers bloom year-round. Another gem is scenic, serene Mounds Park, the bluff-top site of conical burial mounds built by ancient Woodland people. It's the ideal spot to enjoy a panoramic view of downtown St. Paul and the mighty Mississippi River.

Planning Your Visit to the Twin Cities

Contact: Greater Minneapolis Convention & Visitors Association (612/348-7000); St. Paul Convention & Visitors Bureau (800/627-6101; 612/297-6985); Minnesota Office of Tourism (800/657-3700; 612/296-5029).

LODGINGS

Look for chain motels along major freeways such as the I-494 strip. Big hotels abound in downtown Minneapolis, with somewhat fewer in St. Paul.

St. Paul

Chatsworth Bed and Breakfast—This spacious Victorian home is near Grand Avenue shops. Doubles from $75 (612/227-4288).

The Covington Inn—Sleep aboard a renovated towboat anchored along Harriet Island near downtown. Doubles from $105 (612/292-1411).

Radisson Hotel St. Paul—Enjoy panoramic views of the Mississippi. Doubles from $169 (800/333-3333).

The St. Paul Hotel—Find Old World ambience overlooking enchanting Rice Park. Doubles from $175 (800/292-9292).

Minneapolis

Hyatt Regency—From the luxury hotel at the end of Nicollet Mall, follow the walking path to the Loring Park arts area. Doubles from $224 (800/233-1234).

Inn on the Farm—Explore this restored country estate 15 minutes north of downtown, near the world-class Edinburgh USA Golf Course. Doubles from $110 (800/428-8382).

Nicollet Island Inn—A former factory on its own island, the inn is accessible to historic Main St. restaurants and downtown. Doubles from $125 (800/331-6528).

Radisson Hotel Metrodome—Part of the University of Minnesota campus, the hotel offers free shuttle service from 7 a.m. to 11 p.m. to restaurants, sports and shopping within 5 miles. Doubles from $119 (800/822-6757).

Whitney Hotel—Visiting celebrities sometimes choose this eight-story retreat near the Mississippi Mile. Doubles from $160 (800/233-1234).

ST. PAUL DINING

Buca Little Italy—Patrons enjoy hefty family-style portions (612/772-4388).

Carousel—Take the glass elevator 22 stories to view the river from the Radisson Hotel St. Paul (612/292-0408).

Cossetta's Italian Market & Pizzeria—Dine at this downtown eatery and browse its Italian food market and one-of-a-kind shops nearby (612/222-3476).

Dakota Bar & Grill—Regional cuisine and a jazz club earn this nightspot in Bandana Square national acclaim (612/642-1442).

No Wake Cafe—An anchored towboat downtown along Harriet Island serves an eclectic menu (612/292-1411).

St. Paul Grill—American specialties are served in the St. Paul Hotel. The late-night bar menu is perfect after an Ordway performance (612/224-7455).

W.A. Frost & Company—This establishment near the Cathedral charms with a pleasant garden patio in summer and cozy, wood-burning fireplaces in winter (612/224-5715).

Along Grand Avenue—Local dining guides laud these eateries: La Cucaracha (Mexican), Saji-Ya (Japanese), Dixie's (Cajun/Tex-Mex), Lotus (Vietnamese). There's mouth-watering walleye at the Tavern on Grand (612/228-9030) and sinful desserts at Cafe Latté (612/224-5687).

MINNEAPOLIS DINING

Black Forest Inn—Hearty German food and an airy garden patio

make this a choice spot (612/872-0812).
Figlio—This eatery specializes in good food and people-watching at Calhoun Square, a mini-mall and gateway to the Chain of Lakes (612/822-1688).
Gustino's—Operatic servers serenade as they present Italian dishes. Reservations are required at this Marriott City Center location (612/349-4000).
Nicollet Island Inn—Dine on an island overlooking

TOURS

Capital City Trolley—Trolley tours narrate St. Paul's history Monday through Friday—a good buy for 50 cents (612/223-5600).

ATTRACTIONS

Cathedral of St. Paul—Take guided tours Mondays, Wednesdays and Fridays at 1 p.m. (612/228-1766).
James J. Hill House—Stroll through what was one of the Midwest's

samples afterward) at the Home of Pig's Eye Pilsner and Grain Belt Premium in St. Paul (612/290-8209).
Minnesota State Capitol—Free 45-minute guided tours start on the hour (612/296-3962).
St. Paul Gangster Tours—On Saturdays, explore 10 hideouts of America's most notorious gangsters from Ma Barker to John Dillinger. Reservations are required (612/292-1220).

FAMILY FUN

Children's Theatre Company—Attend performances in Minneapolis every month except July and August (612/874-0400).
Como Park is the center of fun: St. Paul's zoo (612/487-8200); amusement rides (612/488-4771); paddleboat, bicycle, canoe rentals (612/489-9311); lakeside concerts, walking paths (612/266-6400).
Historic Fort Snelling—Depicting outpost life in 1827, soldiers perform drills (612/725-2413).
Lake Harriet Bandshell—Enjoy popular summer concerts in Minneapolis (612/661-4875).
Lock and Dam No. 1—Gates redirect river traffic below the Ford Parkway Bridge in St. Paul. Stop at the promenade for an excellent view (612/724-2971).

MINNESOTA ORCHESTRA

The Minnesota Orchestra's Viennese Sommerfest draws music lovers to downtown Minneapolis.

the Mississippi (612/331-3035).
Palomino Euro Bistro—The Hennepin Ave. theater crowd frequents this sophisticated setting (612/339-3800).
Restaurants on SE Main St.—Pracna on Main, built in 1890, features a sidewalk cafe (612/379-3200).
Anthony's Wharf caters to the seafood crowd (612/378-7058). Sip cognac after dark at romantic Sophia (612/379-1111).

largest homes in the 1890s. Reservations are suggested. Saturday walking tours of Summit Ave. (St. Paul) start here, June through September (612/297-2555).
Hubert H. Humphrey Metrodome—Visit the home of the Vikings, Twins and University of Minnesota Golden Gophers football (612/335-3309).
Minnesota Brewing Company—Take a free brewery tour (with

TRAVEL GUIDE

Minnehaha Falls—Hike the wooded glen from the falls in Minnehaha Park to the creek's end at the river in Minneapolis (612/661-4875).

Minnesota Children's Museum—Crawl through a giant anthill or create a thunderstorm in this hands-on center in downtown St. Paul (612/225-6000).

Minnesota Zoo and IMAX 3D Theatre—This zoo in Apple Valley has it all: natural habitats, a tropical rain forest, dolphin shows and Discovery Bay marine education center (800/366-7811). Marvel at the six-story IMAX screen (612/431-4629).

Mounds Park—View St. Paul's barge, train, car and air traffic from ancient burial grounds (612/266-6400).

Padelford Packet Boat Company, Inc.—Cruise on a sternwheel riverboat between Harriet Island and Ft. Snelling and from Boom Island in Minneapolis (612/227-1100).

Science Museum of Minnesota and 3M Omnitheater—Walk under a dinosaur or make a tornado in St. Paul (612/221-9444).

Trains at Bandana Square—An amazing 3,400 square feet of trains travel through reproduced scenes in St. Paul (612/647-9628).

MUSEUMS

American Swedish Institute—This mansion in Minneapolis celebrates Swedish heritage with hundreds of artifacts (612/871-4907).

Frederick R. Weisman Art Museum—Treasure American art in this notable stainless-steel building on the University of Minnesota's east bank (612/625-9494).

Minneapolis Institute of Arts—More than 80,000 artworks include Oriental jade, African masks, Old Masters and French Impressionists (612/870-3131).

Minnesota History Center—This stunning addition to St. Paul's skyline contains a collection ranging from Tiffany glass to Antarctica expedition equipment (800/657-3773).

Walker Art Center and Minneapolis Sculpture Garden—Contemporary art finds a home here, featuring a courtyard with sculptures (612/375-7600).

THEATER

Brave New Workshop—Founded by Dudley Riggs in 1958, this workshop in Minneapolis is known for improvisation, social satire and comedy (612/332-6620).

Fitzgerald Theater—In St. Paul, the Fitzgerald combines music, theater and live broadcasts of *A Prairie Home Companion*

(612/290-1200).

Great American History Theatre—Original works depict regional history. October-May in St. Paul (612/292-4323).

Guthrie Theater—Attend a classic performance in Minneapolis (612/377-2224).

Hey City Theater—This small cabaret theater in downtown Minneapolis presents long-running hits (612/333-9202).

Intriguing shops line Stillwater's riverfront.

Historic State and Orpheum Theatres—For Broadway shows and concerts, make reservations in downtown Minneapolis (612-339-7007).

Jungle Theater—Minneapolis critics and audiences regularly attend (612/822-7063).

Mystery Cafe—Interactive comedy/murder mystery dinner theater has three locations on Friday and Saturday nights (612/566-2583).

Ordway Music Theatre—Modeled on Europe's performance spaces, this setting in St. Paul hosts Broadway shows, the St. Paul Chamber Orchestra and the Minnesota Orchestra (612/282-3000). Park Square Theatre Company—Classic to contemporary works come alive in downtown St. Paul (612/291-7005). Penumbra Theatre— Experience powerful African-American productions in St. Paul (612/224-3180). Theatre de la Jeune Lune—Nationally recognized for originality, this theater enhances the Minneapolis Warehouse District (612/333-6200).

SHOPPING

Mall of America—The largest shopping and entertainment complex in the U.S. is south of the Twin Cities in Bloomington (612/883-8800). The mall offers 3 miles of shopping and attractions including: UnderWater World (612/883-0202) and Knott's Camp Snoopy, a 7-acre indoor theme park (612/883-8555).

CASINOS

Grand Casino Hinckley— This attraction 80 minutes north of downtown St. Paul is open 24 hours (800/472-6321). Mystic Lake Casino-Hotel—The second largest casino in the

U.S. west of Atlantic City is in Prior Lake (800/262-7799).

FESTIVALS

Festival of Nations— In May, multicultural celebrations enliven downtown St. Paul (612/647-0191). Grand Old Day—This June event kicks off summer with crafts and music along St. Paul's Grand Ave. (612/699-0029). A Taste of Minnesota— July brings food and fireworks to the state capitol (612/228-0018). Viennese Sommerfest— The music, food and spirit of Vienna come to life in July outside Orchestra Hall in downtown Minneapolis (612/371-5656). Minneapolis Aquatennial—This 10-day celebration in July lights up the city with lakeside events, parades and fireworks (612/331-8371). Uptown Art Fair— This August event in Minneapolis draws huge crowds (612/673-9081). Renaissance Festival— Experience 16th-century pageantry near Shakopee (612/445-7361).

WINTER EVENTS

Holidazzle Parades— Holiday lights twinkle on fanciful floats on Nicollet Mall nightly during the holiday shopping season. St. Paul Winter Carnival— Rice Park ice sculptures,

parades and winter sports are part of this 10-day celebration—an annual event since 1886. It's downtown in late January (612/223-4700).

OTHER PLACES TO VISIT

Stillwater

Thirty minutes east of St. Paul, Stillwater sits along the St. Croix River. Browse for antiques, crafts and old books in the Victorian downtown. Lunch along the St. Croix at the Dock Cafe (612/430-3770). Relive railroad dining from the late 1940s aboard the Minnesota Zephyr (612/430-3000). Contact: Stillwater Chamber of Commerce (612/439-4001).

Lake Minnetonka

Eleven miles west of Minneapolis, sample the good life along Lake Minnetonka, the metro area's largest lake. Check out the specialty shops along Lake St. then watch the boat traffic as you sip a cool, refreshing drink outdoors at Sunsets (612/473-5253). Test the waters aboard a chartered yacht or take a turn-of-the-century passenger ferry across the lake. Contact: Greater Wayzata Area Chamber of Commerce (612/473-9595).

By Michaeline Zawistowski

RED WING AND LAKE PEPIN

**The river broadens into a
lake here, its shores dotted with
towns well worth exploring.**

Sixty miles south of the Twin Cities, the
Mississippi broadens, spreading out to form
Lake Pepin. Nestled in this deep river valley where
hardwoods shade the steep hills, a dozen villages
flank the Minnesota and Wisconsin sides of the
river. In fall, when the sugar maples go scarlet and
the leaves of the walnut trees gleam like gilt, a
backdrop of color frames the venerable river towns.

Here, both Minnesota-61 and Wisconsin-35 are
posted with the green-and-white signs bearing
captain's wheels that designate the Great River
Road. In towns on each side of the river, restored
hotels, burgeoning antiques shops and galleries
displaying paintings of local wildlife reside in the
shadow of limestone bluffs. In the spring, window
boxes bloom bright pink and red with geraniums
and impatiens.

Welcome to Red Wing

Red Wing, Minnesota, with red brick Italianate
buildings and a population just over 15,000, is the
largest of these river towns. Dakota chiefs who wore
as their symbol "the wing of the wild swan dyed
scarlet" settled here first. Established in 1837 by
missionaries to the Dakotas, the town derives its
name from this ancient Native American heritage.

Using the area's rich clay deposits to manufacture
pipes and pottery, the settlers of Red Wing made
their town a thriving Civil War-era center for river
trade. Before the end of the 19th century, Red Wing
Stoneware was producing water jugs and butter
crocks bearing the town's name and the familiar
outline of a red wing. Sturdy Red Wing shoes
followed soon after, putting the town's name on feet
across the country.

A major wheat-shipping port in the steamboat
era, Red Wing settled into a sleepy serenity for the
first half of the 20th century. Today, with its pottery-
making tradition undergoing a renaissance, the town
thrives again. Blooms cascade from hundreds of
flower baskets that hang from vintage lampposts,
delighting visitors.

Red Wing is cradled between the river and

GREG RYAN

Sailboats at Lake
City Marina on
Lake Pepin.

500-foot-high Barn Bluff. Most visitors say the trek is worth the view at the top of the bluff. (After Henry David Thoreau climbed it in the 19th century, he wrote glowingly about the region's grandeur.)

The city's best-known landmark is the stately, four-story St. James Hotel, built in 1875. Constructed of red brick and highlighted with white trim, the award-winning hotel looks out on the river, occupying most of a city block. Its 60 rooms, each named after a riverboat, wed Victorian ambience with modern amenities. The riverboat theme continues in the hotel's Port of Red Wing Restaurant. A motorized San Francisco cable car, the *Spirit of Red Wing*, departs for narrated tours from the St. James on the hour during summer months.

At the hotel's front desk or at the visitors center in the restored Milwaukee Depot along Levee Street, pick up brochures for three walking tours that showcase the gingerbread architecture Red Wing has worked hard to preserve. The Goodhue County Historical Museum, one of the state's largest, underwent a multimillion dollar renovation in the early '90s. It exhibits everything

Amish Country Quilts & Furniture in Stockholm.

Tour Red Wing's downtown by trolley.

LAYNE KENNEDY

from the tusks of a woolly mammoth to a diorama of Chief Red Wing's Dakota village.

A Heritage of Pottery and Shoes

The restored buildings that house shops and eateries downtown are part of the historic shopping district, including specialty shops in the St. James Hotel and in Riverfront Centre along Main Street. Inside Riverfront Centre are the museum and retail shop of Red Wing Shoe Store, which Cinderella's stepsisters would have loved—it carries shoes from 6 AA (extra narrow) to 16 EEEE (extra wide). Also downtown, the painstakingly restored 1904 Sheldon Theatre hosts national and community theater groups that perform in a jewel-box interior of ivory and gold plaster work.

At the west end of town, the enormous former factory, where wheels and kilns produced Red Wing pottery, now houses an outlet mall. In the same area, visitors can see a revival of two of the seven lines of pottery from Red Wing's turn-of-the-century glory days.

The pottery-making tradition lives on at potter John Falconer's Red Wing Stoneware Co. Here, visitors can tour the factory and observe artisans making both modern items and replicas of antique pottery. Crafting some items by hand, they are adapting the old Red Wing Stoneware's original processes and materials to modern tastes and standards. At the Red Wing Pottery Salesroom, you'll see a display of the original Red Wing pottery and watch today's salt-glazed pottery take shape on the potter's wheel.

Beyond Red Wing

Red Wing is a grand jumping-off point for exploring Lake Pepin, a lovely spot where the Mississippi seems to change character, spreading itself wide to encompass inlets and islands. The romantic waterscape has been compared to scenes along Europe's Rhine River. Dawn mists shroud the lake in mystery. By mid-morning, the sun shines down on waters alive with sailboats.

Outdoor enthusiasts head here for bird-watching, hikes with dizzying, but photogenic heights, as well as cross-country and downhill skiing. Rent a bicycle and pedal along the scenic and popular Cannon Valley Trail, a former Chicago Great Western railroad line that connects Cannon Falls, Welch and Red Wing.

Planning Your Visit to Red Wing

Contact: Red Wing Visitors & Convention Bureau (800/498-3444).

LODGINGS

St. James Hotel—This 1875 Victorian beauty is on the riverfront in downtown Red Wing. Doubles from $80 (800/252-1875).

Best Western Quiet House Suites—This modern motel, with country inn charm and theme rooms, is across the highway from Historic Pottery Place Mall. Doubles from $79 (612/388-1577).

The Candlelight Inn—An authentically decorated Italianate-style home in the heart of the historic district boasts rooms with private baths and fireplaces. Doubles from $85 (800/254-9194).

DINING

Restaurants within the St. James Hotel—A riverboat theme prevails in The Port of Red Wing, located in the lower level of the landmark hotel. Dinner is served year-round and lunch from June to December. The airy Veranda at the back of the shopping court serves breakfast and lunch. Try the Minnesota Wild Rice Soup. A stunning view of the Hiawatha Valley accompanies Sunday brunch

served in the Summit. Clara's bread pudding with hot caramel sauce is named for the plucky girl who began work at the St. James as a waitress and ended up an owner (800/252-1875).

Liberty's Restaurant and Lounge—Antiques and photographs tell the story of Red Wing's heyday. Enjoy live music on weekends and a Friday buffet with chicken, shrimp, meatballs and fish (612/388-8877).

SIGHTSEEING

Walking Tours—On foot is the best way to see the Civil War-era commercial buildings and houses dating to the 1890s. Pick up "Footsteps Through Historic Red Wing" at the St. James Hotel or at the visitors center in the restored Milwaukee Depot along Levee St. Walking tours begin near the river at Levee Park.

Trolley Rides—Join a narrated tour on the Spirit of Red Wing, a motorized San Francisco cable car that departs from the St. James Hotel (612/388-5945).

The Sheldon Theatre— Tour the country's first municipal theater, opened in 1904. A major renovation in the 1980s restored the stunning interior. Also watch a multimedia program about the history of Red

Wing (800/899-5759).

Goodhue County Historical Museum—The museum traces state and regional history from the glacial age. View a collection of Red Wing Pottery and an annex with farm tools and a 1926 Studebaker (612/388-6024).

SHOPPING

Riverfront Centre— Contemporary shops in a historic downtown building include Main Street Toys (612/388-5900), Red Wing Shoe Store (612/388-6233) and Wild Wings, with original paintings, sculpture and decoys (800/793-0677).

Historic Pottery Place Mall—Stroll through the tile and wooden walkways of a renovated pottery factory that houses some 50 antiques stores, specialty shops, and outlets, including Van Heusen, Hush Puppies Factory Direct, Corning/Revere Factory Store and The Wallet Works (612/388-1428).

Red Wing Pottery Salesroom—See a potter hand-decorate salt-glazed pottery. This complex includes a huge selection of pottery, as well as a garden shop, two gift stores and an old-fashioned candy store (800/228-0174).

Red Wing Stoneware— Owner John Falconer and fellow artisans blend modern and traditional techniques to create pottery in this shop at the north end of town (612/388-4610).

Al's Antique Mall—Pick up a guide to area antiques shops (12 in Red Wing and 16 in the surrounding area) at a 12,000-square-foot trove with 100 dealer spaces. Find more antiques stores nearby (888/388-0572).

park's Boathouse Village.

Cannon Valley Trail—Once a train route and now a popular bike and in-line skating trail, it parallels the Cannon River from Cannon Falls to Red Wing. The trail descends 115 feet past wetlands and beneath overhanging cliffs (507/263-0508). Rent a bike at Ripley's Rental near the trail head (612/388-5984).

Pepin Heights Orchards, near Lake City in southeast Minnesota, where fruit trees crown the river bluffs.

OUTDOOR RECREATION

Barn Bluff—Climb up this spot at the end of E. Fifth St. for eagle watching and river views. Reach the top via steps and a trail with markers explaining Red Wing's history and ecology.

Bay Point Park and Boathouse Village— A lighted walking path, open all year, is an ideal spot for river watching. Visitors are fascinated by individual floating boat storage houses that adjust to the river's level by riding up and down on poles at the

Hay Creek Forest— Wildflowers and wildlife thrive along the bluffs and in the woods of Hay Creek, a popular trout fishing stream with trails for equestrians and hikers.

Lock and Dam No. 3— Drive 12 miles north of Red Wing on County-18 to watch the river traffic from a viewing platform.

FESTIVALS

River City Days—Attend an early August blowout with dragon-boat races, grandstand shows, a parade, antique cars, an arts-and-crafts show, ice

cream social, and 5k and 10k runs. Fireworks over the Mississippi provide a rousing finale equal to the Fourth of July (800/762-9516).

ON THE MINNESOTA SIDE OF LAKE PEPIN

Lake City

This town (population: 4,500) proudly claims to be the birthplace of waterskiing. It's the headquarters for boating on Lake Pepin, a naturally formed 3-mile-wide section of the river that stretches for 21 miles. Riverwalk, a pedestrian walkway, offers scenic views of the lake and the orchard-topped bluffs (800/369-4123).

LODGINGS

Lake Pepin Lodge— Beachfront lodging at this motel features whirlpool suites, docks and picnic facilities. Doubles from $69 (612/345-5392).

DINING

The Root Beer Stand— Enjoy homemade root beer at this drive-in built in 1948—so authentic, it still has carhops (612/345-2124).

Chickadee Cottage Tea Room & Restaurant— This vintage home now serves as a tea room, bakery and gift shop (612/345-5155).

Waterman's—Walleye in a special-recipe batter is

a treat at this lakeside eatery (612/345-5353).

OUTDOOR FUN

Bushel & Peck—Pick strawberries, azaleas, zinnias, pumpkins and apples at this Lake City orchard (800/428-7435). **Frontenac State Park— Where Dakota and Fox** nations once hunted and fished, find picnic grounds, 62 campsites, and hiking and skiing trails (612/345-3401). **Hok-Si-La Municipal Park and Campground— This area north of Lake** City is great for hiking, rockhounding, primitive camping and relaxing on the beach (612/345-3855). **Lake City Marina—The** river's largest small-craft marina has 600 boat slips, a public beach and tennis courts (612/345-4211). **Mt. Frontenac Ski Area/ Golf Course—This ski** area claims one of the highest vertical drops in the state. Great views of Lake Pepin enhance the 18-hole golf course (800/488-5826).

Wabasha

Settled in the 1830s, Wabasha's historic downtown makes it a popular base for house-boating, eagle watching and antiquing. Arrowhead Bluffs Museum includes Native American artifacts and Winchester rifle display. The setting

may seem familiar, as the town "starred" in the *Grumpy Old Men* movies. Contact: Wabasha Chamber of Commerce (800/565-4158).

LODGINGS

Anderson House—At this three-story, country-style inn, try the chicken and dumplings, plate-size cinnamon rolls and fudge pie (800/535-5467).

DINING

Wabasha Boatworks and Slippery's Tavern and Restaurant—Dine alfresco on the riverfront (612/565-4748).

SHOPPING

L.A.R.K. Toys and the Meadowlark Shops— In Kellogg, just south of Wabasha, watch artisans carve a carousel within a shopping complex that includes an antique toy museum. Stores sell timeless, amusing objects such as wood carvings, puppets, nesting dolls and puzzles (507/767-3387).

OUTDOOR FUN

Great River Houseboats— See the Mississippi from pontoons, houseboats, fishing boats or runabouts (612/565-3376). **Richard J. Dorer Memorial Hardwood Forest—You'll need a** detailed map to hike the Kruger Unit of the forest, renowned for its

Hikers set up camp at Richard J. Dorer Memorial Hardwood State Forest near Wabasha.

views of the Zumbro River Valley, 5 miles southwest of Wabasha (612/296-6157).

FESTIVALS

Annual Riverboat Days— Wabasha's late July festival includes classic cars, an arts-and-crafts fair and a river run (800/565-4158). Grumpy Old Men Festival—Named for the film that gave new life to an old town, this February fest includes ice fishing and ice-shack contests, dances, raffles and a spaghetti dinner (800/565-4158).

ON THE WISCONSIN SIDE OF LAKE PEPIN

Contact: Wisconsin Tourism (800/432-8747).

Stockholm

Founded in 1854 by Swedish immigrants, the tiny village (population: 89) midway along Lake Pepin's shore is home to several artists. Memorabilia from Swedish settlers fills the Stockholm Museum, formerly an old post office. On the third Saturday in July, artists set up tents in a village park for the annual Stockholm Art Fair (715/442-2419). Stop in to see the herbs and perennials at Stockholm Gardens (715/442-3200).

LODGINGS

The Merchants' Hotel— This 1860s country-style inn, with three guest rooms, adjoins an antiques shop (715/442-2113).

DINING

The Star Cafe—This unexpectedly sophisti-cated restaurant offers a choice of à la carte dining or a five-course meal at a fixed price (715/442-2023).

SHOPPING

Amish Country Quilts and Furniture—Browse through a first-class selection of exquisite Amish quilts and Amish Heritage Furniture in this classic general store (800/247-7657).

Pepin

Pepin pays tribute to its native daughter and the beloved author of the Little House books at Laura Ingalls Wilder Wayside Memorial, a replica of her birthplace. The site, in a park along County-CC, was the setting for Little House in the Big Woods. The Pepin Historical Museum displays Wilder artifacts and rooms furnished in pioneer style (715/442-3011). The third weekend in September brings Laura Ingalls Wilder Days, when the fun includes a Laura look-alike contest

(715/442-3011). Harbor View Cafe—This casual but elegant river-front eatery has merited national attention. Its creative menu changes daily (715/442–3893).

Alma

Main St. parallels the river in this small town (population: 919) that's only two streets wide but 7 miles long (south-east of Stockholm). Watch the river traffic at Lock and Dam No. 4 from Buena Vista Park, atop the natural balcony of 500-foot Twelve Mile Bluff (608/685-3330). Book a room at The Gallery House, where the parlor overlooks the lock and dam (608/685-4975). In fall, head 3 miles north to Rieck's Lake Park, where the obser-vation platform has telescopes for watching the majestic tundra swans from mid-October through November.

Super Sale

Mississippi Valley Partners 85-Mile Garage Sale— Rummagers gather and a party atmosphere prevails the first week-end in May when residents of a dozen villages on both sides of the river clean out their garages and attics (800/369-4123).

By Rebecca Christian

WINONA AND TREMPEALEAU

These Minnesota and Wisconsin river towns are gateways to an unspoiled wilderness.

In 1805, explorer Zebulon Pike wrote rhapsodically about the view from the ridge above present-day Winona, Minnesota: "… at our feet was the valley through which the Mississippi wound itself by numerous channels, forming beautiful islands as far as the eye could embrace the scene. It was altogether so variegated and romantic that a man may scarcely expect to enjoy such a view but twice or thrice in the course of his life."

Amazingly, much of what Pike saw, you can see today. In addition to several city parks with arresting views, there are five state parks and two fish and wildlife refuges in this two-state area (Minnesota and Wisconsin) surrounding Winona.

Fishing streams, marinas and trails attract cyclists, hikers, bird-watchers, anglers and boaters. Canoeists navigate a secluded maze of bays and backwaters. The silence is broken only by the splash of oars through water and the calls of egret and heron. About 200 types of birds nest in or migrate through the valley.

Getting to Know Winona

Approaching Winona (population: 25,400), you'll recognize it by the same landmark that early riverboat captains did. Sugar Loaf Mountain soars 500 feet at the southeast edge of this beautiful city. An 85-foot-high limestone monolith where the Sioux once held ceremonies crowns the mountain. The striking formation appears mysterious when it is eerily lit at night.

The town nestles between the big river and bluffs that are still quarried for their high-quality limestone. The Mississippi here is a labyrinth of channels and islands that Mark Twain dubbed the "Thousand Islands." Lake Winona, which once was the main channel of the river, neatly separates the city from the traffic of US-61 along the bluffs. Almost entirely surrounded by water, Winona appeals to visitors with its natural beauty and man-made attractions.

Founded in 1851 by a steamboat captain, Winona bustled as a river port in the 19th century. Wheat

BOB HURT, ARCHITECTURAL ENVIRONMENTS

Winona lies snugly between the river and the bluffs.

shipping and lumbering created fortunes, and by the turn of the century, it was one of the world's wealthiest cities. Today, Winona thrives as a business and industrial center for southeastern Minnesota.

Remnants of its early wealth live on in architecture more diverse and older than that found in many Heartland cities. Architecture buffs admire the buildings in the town's commercial district, among them a spectacular Prairie School bank. A must-see is the Julius C. Wilkie Steamboat Museum, a full-scale replica of a steamboat. It houses a collection of navigational memorabilia, most notably letters by the steamboat's inventor, Robert Fulton.

Richly colored stained glass, a symbol of the city, is particularly resplendent in the Tiffany glass dome of the lavishly decorated Watkins Products administration building. The direct sales company, which now sells such kitchen staples as vanilla, built its success on a 19th-century liniment that was "good for man or beast."

The architectural grandeur of downtown contrasts agreeably with the modest charm of the city's east-side Polish neighborhood, known for its quirky and colorful yard art. Winona's Polish heritage also is reflected in the statue of St. Stanislaus looking down, remote and benign, from the towers of the St. Stanislaus Kostka Catholic Church.

River Valley Riches

Winona serves as headquarters for the sprawling Upper Mississippi River National Wildlife and Fish Refuge. The refuge spans the wildly beautiful stretch of the river from Wabasha, about 30 miles to Rock Island, Illinois, more than 200 miles downstream. Despite the fact that some 3 million people visit the refuge

The Buehler family runs an orchard near La Crescent.

PERRY STRUSE

On its way to St. Paul, a passenger train parallels the river.

DICK SWIFT

each year, there are lush backwaters so silent, remote and densely inhabited by diverse wildlife that visitors often feel they are the first humans to explore them.

Though some 57 species of mammals, 45 types of amphibians and reptiles, and 188 kinds of fish spend part of their lives at the refuge, it is particularly important as a habitat for birds. Part of the Mississippi Flyway from Canada to the Gulf of Mexico, the refuge is a temporary haven for bald eagles, tundra swans and other birds that use it as a pathway up the continent.

Neighboring Trempealeau

Across the river from Winona are the rocky peaks of Trempealeau Mountain, a striking island bluff created when an ancient river changed its course. Today's river makes a bend at the village of Trempealeau, Wisconsin. In this town (population: 1,039), modest, contemporary homes mix with a few old Victorian storefronts in what has become western Wisconsin's laid-back headquarters for outdoor recreation. Hikers, bikers, birders and canoeists head to the region to enjoy well-

marked trails in a vast, unspoiled setting.

At the Historic Trempealeau Hotel, an unornamented 1871 frame building, you can rent a room or sample the grilled fish in the sunny dining room. (The hotel offers luxury suites with river views in a nearby historic home.)

On the south side of Trempealeau is Lock and Dam No. 6, where visitors watch the river traffic from an elevated and covered observation stand. Tows of barges as vast and cumbersome as prehistoric beasts pass through the lock.

The best place to view Trempealeau Mountain is from Brady's Bluff in Perrot State Park at the edge of the Mississippi. There are ancient petroglyphs and two trails that head up the bluff, winding past a prairie riotous with seasonal color.

The Great River State Bicycle Trail links the park with the Trempealeau National Wildlife Refuge. The 5,600-acre refuge is a major stopover for migrating herons and egrets. Bald eagles nest here, too. To experience it all up close, follow the marked canoe trail that starts at the nature center, then snakes through the backwater channels of the Trempealeau River. You may feel as adventurous as Zebulon Pike.

Planning Your Visit to Winona and Trempealeau

Contact: Winona Convention & Visitors Bureau (800/657-4972); Trempealeau Chamber of Commerce (608/534-6780).

LODGINGS

Carriage House Bed & Breakfast—An elegant three-story carriage house built by a 19th-century Winona lumber baron boasts four guest rooms, three with gas fireplaces. Doubles from $80 (507/452-8256).

Best Western Riverport Inn & Suites—This sparkling modern motel with theme rooms offers a good view and miles of walkway across the street at Lake Park. Doubles from $79 (507/452-0606).

Trempealeau Hotel—Serving travelers as a restaurant and saloon since 1871, this easy-going old river town hotel has bike and canoe rentals and a summer concert series. Eight rooms have shared baths. There's also a restored home with two luxury suites. Doubles from $30 (608/534-6898).

DINING

Bloedow's Bakery—Since 1924, Winonans have enjoyed bread, doughnuts and cookies at this east-end bakery (507/452-3682).

Hot Fish Shop—A family-owned favorite in Winona since the 1930s, the shop features batter-fried walleye pike and other fried or broiled fish. See the Aquarium Room, and waltz and polka in the Fisherman's Lounge Tuesdays–Saturdays (507/452-5002).

Jefferson Pub & Grill—A railroad freight house converted to a casual restaurant, this affordable eatery is along the river in downtown Winona near the steamboat museum (507/452-2718).

The Bun Barn—Enjoy soups, salads and make-your-own sandwiches from homemade bread and a variety of meats and cheeses at this downtown establishment. Try homemade pies, cookies and cakes, too (507/452-5700).

Ed Sullivan's—Along the river between Trempealeau and Perrot State Park, this family eatery serves hearty portions. There's an Irish theme, with Emerald Isle specialties such as brown bread muffins and crusty potatoes. The restaurant has a shuttle to the Trempealeau Marina (608/534-7775).

SIGHTSEEING

Julius C. Wilkie Steamboat Museum—This downtown Winona museum replicates a steamboat, with a second-floor Grand Salon decorated in glorious Victorian excess (507/454-1254).

Polish Cultural Institute of Winona—The local history and folklore of the largest concentration of Kashubian Poles in the U.S. are on display in the former lumber company, where many of the area's Polish immigrants once worked (507/454-3431).

Winona Armory Museum—This 1915 brick fortress houses one of the largest historical society museums in Minnesota. It has stained-glass windows, library archives, a gift shop and a used bookstore (507/454-2723).

Watkins Buildings—At the Watkins Heritage Museum & Store, learn about liniments and tonics. Or order today's Watkins products such as spices and vanilla extract (507/457-6095). The Watkins Administration Building is a two-story, block-long blend of classical Viennese- and Prairie School-style architecture (507/457-3300). The lavishly decorated Tudor-style Watkins Home offers tours by appointment (507/454-4670).

Walking tours—Experience Winona's architecture. Pick up a brochure at the visitors bureau at 67 Main St.

SHOPPING

Winona Knits, Inc.— One of America's oldest and largest sweater and sportswear retailers has a shop at the foot of Sugar Loaf (507/454-1724).

Winona Gallery Outlet Store—Purchase embroidered and screen-printed clothing at discount prices, plus crafts from tri-state-area

Venture on the Great River Road on the Wisconsin or Minnesota side of the Mississippi for exceptional scenery.

artisans (507/454-8801).

Heart's Desire Gifts— For lace, potpourri, cards, gourmet foods and other gift items, stop by this landmark Gothic Revival bank building (507/452-5621).

Winona Farmers Market—Ask about the current location of this market, where local farmers sell flowers, vegetables, herbs and baked goods on Wednesday afternoons and Saturday mornings from mid-May–September

(608/525-6701).

Montoville Antiques & Fine Crafts—Trempealeau's Information Center displays folk art, Adirondack furniture, vintage jewelry, handmade porcelain dolls, baskets and driftwood birdhouses (608/534-6780).

OUTDOOR RECREATION

Request guides from the Winona Convention & Visitors Bureau for bicycle routes and canoe routes, as well as cross-country ski and snowmobile trails.

Garvin Heights Park— Hike and picnic in the center of town at this city park, with a scenic drive and an overlook with a panoramic view of the river. Drive south on Huff St., past the junction of US-14 and US-61.

Sugar Loaf—Towering over Lake Winona, the unusual formation on top of a bluff was a landmark for riverboat pilots. In east Winona, it's above the junction of US-14,

US-61 and State-43.

Lake Park—A jogging and walking path, 18-hole disk golf, volleyball sand pits, fishing piers and a rose garden are among the amenities of this city park along Lake Winona, between Huff St. and Mankato Ave.

Winona Aquatic Center—For a refreshing dip, try the Olympic-size pool and zero-depth municipal pool with its 208-foot water slide. Or join in a game on the sand volleyball court (507/457-8210).

Upper Mississippi River National Wildlife and Fish Refuge—More than 260 miles long and up to 3 miles wide, the refuge has an astonishing variety of wildlife. The birds number among the largest populations in the country, even year-round. Canoeing and primitive camping are popular in this sanctuary (507/452-4232).

Great River Bluffs State Park (formerly O.L. Kipp State Park)—Looking out on the Mississippi River, this park offers camping, including a new bicycle-only campground, 16 miles southeast of Winona (507/643-6849).

Perrot State Park— Set at the junction of the Mississippi and Trempealeau rivers, the park boasts hiking and cross-country ski trails, stunning river valley views, camping and a nature center (608/534-6409).

Great River State Bicycle Trail—A 24-mile scenic corridor through the backwaters of the Mississippi affords photography and snowmobiling opportunities. The trail connects with 100 miles of the State Bicycle Trail corridor, which includes the La Crosse River and Elroy-Sparta trails to the south (608/534-6409).

Locks and Dams—At No. 5, there are a wayside area and viewing stand, 13 miles west of Winona, just off US-61. At No. 6, more than 2,000 small pleasure boats pass through annually. Watch from an enclosed observation tower on the south side of Trempealeau.

Big Valley Ranch, Inc.— Schedule horseback riding daily by appointment near Winona (507/454-3305).

Trempealeau Marina— Find houseboat rentals, docks and a launch ramp near Perrot State Park and the Trempealeau National Wildlife Refuge (608/534-6033).

ANNUAL EVENTS

Trempealeau Chamber of Commerce Bike Tour— Choose from 10-, 25- or 50-mile rides of varying levels of difficulty that begin in downtown Trempealeau, follow the river and continue in Perrot State Park the second Saturday in May (608/534-6780).

Winona Downtown Arts & River Fest—Festivities include fireworks over the Mississippi, carriage rides, arts, crafts and a lighted boat regatta in late June (507/452-2281).

Steamboat Days— Celebrate Independence Day with contests, an art show, food fair, fireworks and a carnival the first week in July (800/657-4972).

Trempealeau Catfish Days—On the first weekend after July Fourth, 15,000 folks

Oktoberfest in LaCrosse, Wisconsin, brings parades, polkas and plenty of bratwursts and beer.

turn out for a parade, flea market and run (608/534-6780).

Victorian Fair—Old-time music, food and festivities, and demonstrations by craftspeople take place the last weekend in September (507/454-2723).

Winona Wildlife Weekend—Wildlife painters and regional artists display their works in late October (507/452-2272).

Swan Watch—This two-day event in early November includes a field trip to view migrating tundra swans along the Mississippi (800/657-4972).

OTHER PLACES TO VISIT
La Crescent, Minnesota

Visit the self-proclaimed apple capital of Minnesota. Situated on a crescent-shaped piece of land that narrows the river's channel, La Crescent has ridges with rocky soil that gives apples intense flavor. The river safeguards the area's 800 acres of orchards from early chills. To view the orchards in bloom, head out of La Crescent on County-29, a State Scenic Byway that is part of the Hiawatha Trail. The narrow blacktop road gradually inclines almost 1,000 feet, past the contoured fields of farms and up to blufftop orchards.

Leidel's Apples—At this stop along State-16 in La Crescent, choose from more than 20 varieties of apples at one of the region's biggest and oldest orchards (507/895-4832).

Applefest—Arrive in mid-September and join the 50,000 visitors who turn out for this annual celebration that dates back to the 1940s. Enjoy a parade, orchard tours, carnival and the not-to-be-missed aroma of 1,000 freshly baked pies (507/895-2800). Contact: La Crescent Chamber of Commerce (507/895-2800).

La Crosse, Wisconsin

Wisconsin's largest river city (population: 51,000), fun-loving, hard-working La Crosse is a half-hour drive south of Winona. In the 1700s, it was a major rendez-vous site for traders and Native Americans. The city's lumbering and brew-making heritage comes alive in narrated river cruises and brewery tours. Contact: La Crosse Area Convention & Visitors Bureau (800/658-9424).

LODGINGS

Lumber Baron Inn Bed & Breakfast—Borrow a complimentary bike and cycle the Great River Bike Trail to work off the gourmet breakfast you'll be served in this trailside Victorian bed and breakfast. This inn in Onalaska, overlooking the Black River, is in the National Register of Historic Places. Doubles from $69 (608/781-8938).

Radisson Hotel—Located along the Mississippi River in downtown La Crosse, the hotel is near the Great River Steamboat Company. Doubles from $109 (608/784-6680).

DINING

Casablanca—Sample acclaimed Middle-Eastern cuisine in a small dining room with homelike atmosphere in Onalaska. Reservations required (608/783-7880).

Rudy's—Roller-skating carhops take you back to the '50s at this La Crosse drive-in, where draft root beer is brewed daily (608/782-2200).

Piggy's Restaurant—The food and the river view are more elegant than the name of this award-winning restaurant in La Crosse. It specializes in steaks, barbecue and seafood (608/784-4877).

SIGHTSEEING AND RECREATION

G. Heileman Brewery—View the world's largest six-pack and high-tech brewing at this longtime brewery in La Crosse (608/782-2337).

The Great River Steamboat Company—Take sightseeing cruises and one- or two-day excursions on the *Julia Belle Swain,* one of only a few steam-powered boats still operating on the Mississippi River (800/815-1005).

Fun 'n the Sun Houseboat Vacations—Glide out of the home port of La Crosse in a houseboat complete with its own water slide. The luxury boats sleep six to 12. Rates from $850 for four nights (608/783-7326).

FESTIVALS

Mississippi Log Boom—Nationally televised American Lumberjack Championships, a rendezvous and the primitive camps of skilled artisans recall fur trading and logging eras in La Crosse's Pettibone Park in early August (800/658-9424).

Oktoberfest—La Crosse hosts one of the Midwest's largest German festivals, with 7 days of musical entertainment, sporting events, food and crafts, and a torchlight parade in late September and early October (608/784-3378).

By Rebecca Christian

BLUFF COUNTRY

Anyone who thinks the Heartland is flat land will be astonished by the countryside along the Mississippi River. Winding roads lead to towering tree-shaded bluffs, and towns large and small climb the hillsides or nestle in hollows along the river.

The Mississippi is a powerful sight from blufftop or dockside, but to really understand the river, you'll need to venture on the water. Rent a houseboat and you're in charge, maneuvering past massive strings of barges and skirting solitary wooded islands. When the spirit strikes, you can tie up at a small town waterfront and go exploring. As the sun goes down, choose a sandy shore and cook your dinner over a campfire.

For a taste of 19th-century travel, consider journeying on the river the way the Midwest's early settlers did—by steamboat. Paddle-wheelers still ply the Mississippi, and you can choose a two-hour jaunt or take a two-week cruise with your own cozy stateroom each night.

If your Mississippi River fantasy involves drifting downriver in the afternoon sun with a fishin' pole in hand, ask about boat rentals or fishing charters at any town along the river that strikes your fancy. In some areas, the backwaters that feed the big river are navigable, and renting a canoe will allow you to paddle your way through slender reeds to a hidden world of egrets and otters.

Once you're back on land, Ole Man River will seem like a longtime friend who has shared your adventure, a companion you'll always be happy to meet again.

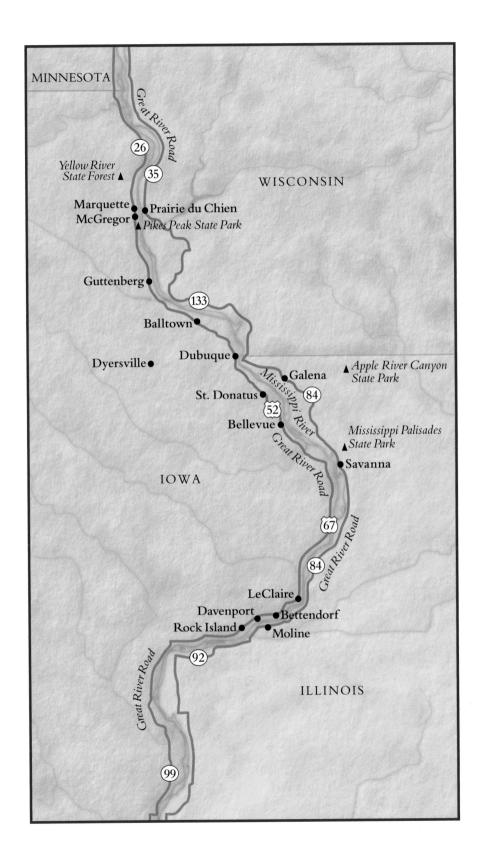

FROM MARQUETTE TO GUTTENBERG

Life slows to an easy pace aboard a houseboat, the ideal way to experience the river.

There's no better spot for contemplating the timeworn character of the Mississippi's rugged bluffs than from the river itself. Seen in changing light from dawn to dusk from the deck of your own houseboat, the river and its shoreline become an indelible memory.

Northeast Iowa is prime houseboating territory. The glaciers never leveled this corner of the state, sometimes called "Little Switzerland" because of its roller-coaster roads and Old World landscape of forests and farmland. From Lansing, near the Minnesota state line, down to the staunchly Germanic town of Guttenberg, Iowa is anything but flat. Roads snake past looming limestone bluffs, dense woods and backwaters, where the only sounds are the hum of insects, the call of birds and the rhythmic slice of a kayaker's paddle through the dark water. Quaint towns along the river's path invite exploration.

Houseboat enthusiasts sing the praises of a vacation experience that combines the comfort of a dwelling and the freedom of a water craft. Sitting on deck and savoring the morning's first cup of coffee, with only the soft splash of a fish breaking the stillness of the sunrise, make the workaday world disappear.

Bob Myers, owner of Boatels Houseboat Rentals in McGregor, Iowa, a half-century-old family-run business, sees it happen all the time. "People come from Chicago or the East or West Coast, from the city's mad rush, get out on a houseboat and totally slow down."

Before he gently shoves houseboats away from the shore and waves farewell, Bob gives his amateur pilots a lesson in Houseboating 101: how to maneuver the 46- to 52-foot vessels when a string of barges approaches. He also tells boaters about landmarks such as Clayton's Lite House, 10 miles downriver in the historic fishing village of Clayton. Here, houseboaters can pull up to the dock for a catfish dinner.

The houseboats' home port, McGregor (population: 800) is one of several former frontier outposts along this stretch of the river road. McGregor began as a ferry-boat landing, then became a Civil War-era center for

DOUG SMITH

The town of
McGregor, Iowa,
lures boaters
ashore.

storing and shipping grain from rich Iowa farmlands to the west. With 30 saloons along its shoreline, it was a popular stop for thirsty 19th-century riverboat crews.

Today, many of McGregor residents' livelihoods still depend on the river. Flashlights in hand, youngsters earn pocket money by digging for nightcrawlers after dusk, then advertising them the next day with hand-lettered yard signs. Marinas and bait shops dot the waterfront. Even the convenience stores sell smoked perch.

Some houseboaters snooze until noon, then spend the long afternoons river-watching from lounge chairs. More ambitious travelers seek out hiking and biking trails, riding stables and canoe rentals. Wildlife abounds, with good bird-watching and hunting in season.

Hunting of another kind brings visitors to the treasure-packed antiques shops that line McGregor's old-time Main Street. Nowhere is the turn-of-the-century atmosphere more evident than at the River Junction Trade Co. In a vintage building with a tin ceiling and potbellied stove, shelves hold 19th-century clothing and

equipment so scrupulously accurate that River Junction does a thriving mail-order business with people whose hobby is historic reenactments. Hollywood comes calling, too, buying authentic artifacts for Western movies.

Ancient Sites

At Effigy Mounds National Monument in nearby Harpers Ferry, forests of oaks and maples cloak centuries-old Native American burial mounds. Long ago, people of the Upper Mississippi Valley created ceremonial mounds, called effigies, by shaping the earth to resemble the creatures they saw around them— falcons, deer, turtles and especially bears.

At the visitors center, view a film about the meaning of the mounds and how they were built, then head outside to explore. Detecting animal shapes in these low-relief mounds requires some imagination, like recognizing constellations.

Just to the north of McGregor is the little town of Marquette (population: 400), named for a 17th-century Jesuit priest who traveled the Midwest with

Houseboating on the Upper Mississippi.

DOUG SMITH

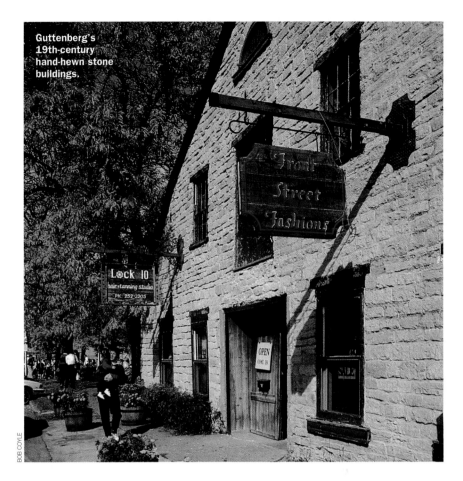

Guttenberg's 19th-century hand-hewn stone buildings.

explorer Louis Joliet. Here the *Miss Marquette Riverboat Casino* docks at the riverfront, making one cruise a day.

Pikes Peak, the highest point along the Mississippi, is 2 miles south of McGregor. It overlooks the site where Joliet and his crew glided through the mouth of the Wisconsin River in 1673, becoming the first Europeans to view the Upper Mississippi. The overlook—voted the most scenic view in a 12-state survey by *Midwest Living* magazine—lies within Pikes Peak State Park. The Northeast Iowa Bike Route, a paved trail that links three state parks, connects Pikes Peak to Guttenburg.

On the Road To Guttenberg

The river road from McGregor to Guttenberg dips inland, running along-side cornfields and past farms where placid cows gather outside weathered red barns. But the road always returns to the river, providing glimpses of the water as it ribbons its way through tunnels of trees. Toward Guttenberg, the view opens up and the road straightens out dramatically, giving a postcard view of the little town so German in its heritage that streets are named after literary giants Goethe and Schiller.

Settled in the mid-1850s, Guttenberg (two "T"s) is named for Johannes Gutenberg (one "T"), the inventor of movable type. The town library displays a replica of a Gutenburg Bible. Walking tours take visitors past pre-Civil War buildings made of hand-hewn stone.

Downtown, the Lockmaster's House Heritage Museum, the last such house along the Upper Mississippi, is a National Register structure next door to Lock and Dam No. 10. Visitors line the observation deck to watch heavily laden barges journeying down from St. Paul or up from Baton Rouge, Louisiana, as they thread their way carefully through the needle's eye of the narrow lock.

TRAVEL GUIDE

Planning Your Visit to Bluff Country

Contact: McGregor/ Marquette Chamber of Commerce (800/896-0910); Guttenberg Civic & Commerce Club (319/252-2323).

LODGINGS

Little Switzerland Inn— Rooms overlook the river in this 1862 building, originally home to one of Iowa's oldest weekly newspapers. Guests also may rent a mid-1800s log cabin next to the inn. Doubles from $65 (319/873-2057).

Holiday Shores Motel— Location is everything for this tidy 33-room modern motel with an indoor pool at the river's edge in McGregor. Doubles from $45 (319/873-3449).

Old Brewery—A bed and breakfast and an art gallery specializing in Iowa scenes bring new life to an old landmark, a stone brewery at the base of a bluff in Guttenberg. Doubles from $55 (319/252-2094; 800/353-1307).

CAMPING

(See listings for Pikes Peak State Park and Yellow River State Forest under Outdoor Recreation, page 47.)

DINING

Captain's Reef Buffet— Locals recommend this bountiful buffet for breakfast, lunch, dinner and nightly entertainment aboard the *Miss Marquette Riverboat Casino.* The boat cruises once a day in summer and has a fourth-floor observation deck (319/873-3531).

Alexander Cafe—In the newly renovated 1899 Alexander Hotel along Main Street in McGregor, the cafe offers big, old-fashioned breakfasts, home-style soups and pies, and a Friday night fish fry in a casual setting (319/873-3838).

White Springs Supper Club—Rustic and reasonable describe this roadside eatery on Business-18 in McGregor. Try the homemade smoked ribs (319/873-9642).

Clayton Lite House— Pull your boat up to the dock of this relaxing restaurant, known for catfish. It's at the water's edge in Clayton, 10 miles south of McGregor (319/964-2103).

SIGHTSEEING

Effigy Mounds National Monument—The Yellow River divides the sprawling 1,481 acres of National Park Service-operated land 3½ miles north of Marquette. Stop at the visitors center to view a film or tour the museum. There are guided tours in summer or you can hike a self-guided trail with markers that explain the prehistoric Native-American mounds and offer river views. Programs include early-morning bird walks and moonlight hikes in summer. Wear appropriate shoes (319/873-3491).

AgriGrain Marketing Tour—From mid-March to the end of November, watch workers load barges with grain and soybeans before shipping them out to

Vintage buildings add to McGregor's riverfront charm.

LARRY KNUTSON

the Gulf of Mexico, where they will be exported to other countries at the rate of 28 million bushels of corn and 12 million bushels of soybeans a year (319/873-3436).

Lockmaster's House Heritage Museum—The last lockmaster house on the Upper Mississippi is a National Register treasure where visitors learn about the engineering system that makes the river navigable for barge traffic, then see the system in action from the observation deck of the lock and dam (319/252-2323).

SHOPPING

Color Me Country— Browse through antique linens, clothes, trunks and a large selection of Boyd bears, along McGregor's old-fashioned Main St. (319/873-2063).

Main Street Mall— More than a dozen dealers sell antique china, glassware, furniture and collectibles in McGregor (319/873-2807; 319/233-0448).

River Junction Trade Co.—Even nonshoppers enjoy a stroll through this authentic turn-of-the-century general store specializing in frontier-era clothing and equipment

(319/873-2387).

Kann Imports—This distinctive, long-established gift store draws visitors to the river's edge in Guttenberg. High-end imports from 75 countries includes Spanish Lladro porcelain, Austrian crystal, a large selection of German beer steins and a year-

Houseboating vacationers will find plenty of opportunities to come ashore for beach picnics.

round Christmas room (319/252-2072).

Farmers Market—Look for this local favorite in Guttenberg on Saturday mornings from Memorial Day through Labor Day.

OUTDOOR RECREATION

Boatels Houseboat Rentals & Marine—This long-established family business in McGregor rents houseboats that sleep 8 to 12. Three- to seven-day rentals from $518 (800/747-2628).

S & S Houseboat Rentals—A fleet of 10 houseboats in Lansing

(11 miles from the Minnesota state line) offers three- to seven-day trips from $636 (800/728-0131).

Landing 615—Cruise below Lock No. 10 on pontoons and fishing boats from this marina in Guttenberg (319/252-1717).

Pikes Peak State Park—One of the highest bluffs along the

entire length of the Mississippi provides a panoramic view of the confluence of the Mississippi and Wisconsin rivers. You'll find hiking trails, picnic tables at the edge of the bluffs and 77 campsites (319/873-2341).

Yellow River State Forest—Just south of Harpers Ferry, this unspoiled preserve of some 9,000 densely wooded acres offers two campgrounds, an equestrian stable, and spring-fed tributaries and trout streams that beckon anglers (319/586-2254).

Northeast Iowa Bike Route—Steep hills make this lovely but challenging bike route an option for seasoned cyclists only. It links Wapsipinicon, Pikes Peak and Backbone state parks. The route also connects Pikes Peak to Guttenberg via X-56, the Great River Road (515/281-5145).

FESTIVALS

Spring Arts and Crafts Festival—Memorial Day Weekend; Fall Arts and Crafts Festival—first full weekend in October. Both are held in Triangle Park and accompanied by a flea market under the bridge in Marquette.

Stars and Stripes River Days—Join in old-fashioned fun in Guttenberg the weekend prior to July Fourth, with food vendors, a flea market, a carnival, games, a parade and a street dance. A Sunday night water-ski show topped by fireworks over the river is the grand finale.

German Fest— Guttenberg's heritage shines on the third weekend of September with German music, folk dancing, food, a parade and even a Hummel look-alike contest.

ON THE WISCONSIN SIDE OF THE RIVER

Contact: Prairie du Chien Area Chamber of Commerce (800/732-1673).

Prairie du Chien and Cassville

A flourishing fur trading post in the 1690s, Prairie du Chien is Wisconsin's second-oldest settlement, after Green Bay. Set at the western tip of the Fox-Wisconsin Waterway across the river from Marquette, the town's strategic location made it important to both Indians and white settlers. Wisconsin's first millionaire, Hercules Dousman, amassed a fortune in the fur trade, then built a gracious home

overlooking the river. Over the years Prairie du Chien, which today has a population of 5,700, was also a site for British and American forts. Just south is Cassville (population: 1,144), a village known for its ferryboat operation and historic sites.

LODGINGS

Best Western Quiet House—With themed whirlpool suites and an indoor pool, this clean, inviting motel is located at the junction of US-18 and State-35. Doubles from $73 (800/528-1234).

DINING

Kaber's Supper Club— This traditional Prairie du Chien supper club is famous for its catfish

Pikes Peak State Park offers an eagle's-eye view of the confluence of the Mississippi and Wisconsin rivers.

DOUG SMITH

STATE HISTORICAL SOCIETY OF WISCONSIN

In Prairie du Chien, Wisconsin, guides at the Villa Louis mansion show a young visitor a Victorian high-wheeler.

19th-century life (608/326-6960).

Wyalusing State Park— Rock formations, steep valleys and lookouts give character to the hiking trails in this 2,700-acre park at the confluence of the Mississippi and Wisconsin rivers. A marked canoe route winds through the river islands. The park includes picnic areas and 110 campsites (608/996-2261).

Cassville Car Ferry— The ferry takes travelers with or without cars between Millville, Iowa, and Cassville, 4 miles south of Guttenberg on US-52; watch for signs (608/725-5180).

Stonefield Historic Village and Nelson Dewey State Park— Pass through a covered bridge to explore more than 30 buildings and vintage farm machinery in this re-creation of a turn-of-the-century farming village (608/ 725-5210). The site is adjacent to Nelson Dewey State Park, on the grounds of the Civil War-era home of the state's first governor, for whom it is named. With wooded campsites and good river views, the park is a prime eagle-watching spot in winter (608/725-5374).

fry (608/326-6216).

Jeffers Black Angus— For a pleasant evening out, dine at this restaurant specializing in steaks and seafood in Prairie du Chien (608/326-2222).

SIGHTSEEING

Villa Louis—Visit this opulent 1870 Italianate brick mansion on St. Feriole Island on the Mississippi. Knowledgeable guides show off this historic complex with a fine collection of furnishings from the home's original owners. Each September, handsome teams of horses, polished

carriages, and riders and drivers enliven the grounds during the Villa Louis Carriage Classic. The Astor Fur Trade Museum and Museum of Prairie du Chien are on the grounds of the mansion, which is open daily May 1–October 31 (608/326-2721).

Prairie du Chien Museum at Fort Crawford—Exhibits in the restored 1831 Fort Crawford hospital reflect frontier days when civilians, Native Americans and soldiers inhabited Prairie du Chien. Each September, a military camp allows visitors to experience

By Rebecca Christian

DUBUQUE

Cable cars, cobblestones and big-screen notoriety make this Iowa city a standout.

BOB COYLE

Dubuque, Iowa's oldest city, crowns one of the loveliest stretches along the Great River Road. The towers and turrets of venerable red brick buildings rise above the Mississippi River's limestone bluffs at Dubuque. Here, people and nature have created an enchanting cityscape.

The 60,000 residents of this old German-Irish city enjoy flaming foliage in the fall, cross-country and downhill skiing in winter, and hiking trails, riverboat gambling and rich history year-round. Dubuque and the hilly area around it are so striking they have served as the backdrop for several movies, among them *Field of Dreams*. Part of the attraction for Hollywood is the yesteryear look created by the lack of TV antennas. The bluffs make it impossible for residents to get television reception without cable, so Dubuque retains its pristine Victorian skyline.

The city is named for Julien Dubuque, an intrepid French-Canadian fur trader who mined the area's rich lead resources in the 18th century. Today, the Julien Dubuque Monument towers over his grave on a bluff that commands the Mississippi. The striking monument is part of the Mines of Spain Recreation Area, a sprawling park and National Historic Landmark with remnants of 19th-century lead mines. The area's nature trails, limestone quarry, interpretive center and most of all, changing landscape—from dense glades and wetlands to prairies brilliant with wildflowers—make it popular for scenic drives.

Charming Cable Cars

In this city of landmarks, the most distinctive may be the Fenelon Place Elevator, a much-photographed symbol of Dubuque. The green-and-white cable car bills itself as the world's shortest and steepest railway. Riders board at its base in a namesake area of antiques and specialty shops called Cable Car Square. The district echoes with the clip-clop of horses' hooves as carriages of visitors move smartly along the cobblestone streets.

The wooden cable car owes its existence to a siesta-loving Victorian-era banker. He liked to nap at lunch but couldn't afford the time because of the long buggy ride between the business district and his blufftop home. His solution was a European-style incline railway that affords today's visitors a

Catch an exhilarating view of Dubuque from a paddle wheeler.

RT OF DUBUQUE

magnificent view of Iowa, Wisconsin and Illinois. Cyclists board with their bikes for the trip up the hill, then pedal leisurely back down.

From the top of Fenelon Place, you'll see a slender brick tower in the distance. In Civil War days, the Old Shot Tower was where workers turned lead into grapeshot for ammunition. Located close by is the Dubuque Brew Pub, the oldest brewery in Iowa, which serves award-winning micro brews with the Dubuque Star label.

On the Waterfront

One of the best places to experience a river city is along the waterfront, an area that's too hardworking and industrial to be merely pretty. Still a busy river port, Dubuque once was one of the most important boat-building cities along the Mississippi.

Dubuque's Ice Harbor is home to a museum complex, an antiques-and-craft mall in a restored factory, a floating casino and a nongambling boat for sightseeing. The Mississippi River Museum, one of the largest river museums in the country, covers six sites that provide an overview of Dubuque and the river. A good place to start is the River of Dreams Theater. Here, visitors view a state-of-the-art film about the Mississippi. It's shown on two screens flanked by illuminated, three-dimensional artifacts such as a vintage bathing suit.

The complex also includes a museum in which guests enter a lead mine, a historic side-wheeler with living quarters authentically rigged for workers, a 1940 towboat and a boatyard where the famous Dubuque boats once were built.

Dubuque's downtown is a living museum of restored churches, theaters and mansions. St. Luke's United Methodist Church, the oldest church in Iowa, welcomes visitors who come to gaze at the rich and subtle colors of its legendary stained-glass windows, created by Louis C. Tiffany.

Victorian rooftops crown Dubuque's river bluffs.

BOB COYLE

Dubuque's unique cable-car system.

Fenelon Place Elevator Co.

FARE ADULTS ONE WAY 50¢ ROUND TRIP 1.00 CHILDREN 5-12 YRS 25¢ ROUND TRIP BIKE & RIDER ONE WAY 60¢

HOURS 8:00 A.M. to 10:00 P.M.

Visit the same neighborhood on Saturday morning to experience nature's artistry. For generations, farmers have been bringing colorful produce and flowers to the Farmers Market here from May to October.

Prominent on the city's cultural landscape are two turn-of-the-century theaters, Five Flags (an old vaudeville house) and the Grand Opera House, home to community productions, as well as traveling shows. The Dubuque Museum of Art, a National Historic Landmark in the shadow of the county courthouse's glittering gold dome, is a rare example of Egyptian Revival architecture.

Bird-watchers, hikers and cyclists frequent the river valley for its natural beauty. Many cities along the river have an Eagle Point Park; Dubuque's is a classic that overlooks General Zebulon Pike Lock and Dam No. 11. Its handsome horizontal shelters are made of native stone in the Frank Lloyd Wright style. Located near the park is the Tollbridge Inn, a restaurant with a panoramic view of the river traffic and stylish live piano music—the better to view it by. Near the park entrance is the Mathias Ham House, a restored mansion that captures the flavor of life in the steamboating era.

On the northern outskirts of town, Heritage Trail, a converted railroad bed, meanders along 26 miles of rock outcroppings and streams, making it a favorite with fossil hunters, hikers, bikers, snowmobilers and cross-country skiers. West of Dubuque, Sundown Mountain Ski Area has 22 runs. Nearby is one of the area's most inviting lodgings, Juniper Hill Bed & Breakfast. Also to the west is Dubuque Arboretum and Botanical Gardens, which boasts award-winning All-America rose gardens and the world's largest hosta glade.

Planning Your Visit to Dubuque

Contact: Dubuque Convention & Visitors Bureau (800/798-8844; http://www.dubuque.org).

LODGINGS

You'll find a choice of chain motels along US-20 west of town. Ask at the visitors bureau for a list of lodgings.

The Mandolin Inn— This Queen Anne-style mansion downtown has eight rooms and serves a sumptuous breakfast in a dining room with a striking original mural. Doubles from $75 (800/524-7996).

Juniper Hill Farm— A sprawling, shingled Scottish-style cottage west of town near Sundown Mountain Ski Area, this sunny bed and breakfast with an outdoor hot tub and three large guest rooms is pure country. Fruits grown on the farm go into the breads and syrups served at breakfast. Doubles from $80 (800/572-1449).

DINING

Shot Tower Inn—Locals swear by the pizza at this very casual eatery near Cable Car Square. Try the mini-taco appetizers (319/556-1061).

The Tollbridge Inn— "Finest Dining by a Dam Site" is the motto for this white-tablecloth restaurant near Eagle Point Park. It features scampi and prime rib, live music and a panoramic view of river traffic at the lock and dam below (319/556-5566).

SIGHTSEEING

Fenelon Place Elevator— This quaint cable car makes a sheer vertical climb up a limestone bluff April through November (319/582-6496).

Dubuque Brew Pub— Big, full-flavored micro brews are on tap at Iowa's oldest brewery, located by the landmark Shot Tower. The pub is open year-round, with seasonal hours in fall and winter (319/583-1218).

The Mississippi River Museum—A complex of six sites, it includes a towboat and a channel dredger. The hands-on museum gives a comprehensive overview of the city and the vast water highway that shaped its destiny (800/226-3369).

Diamond Jo Casino— Located in the Ice Harbor, the casino boasts a dining room and three levels of gaming. One early-morning cruise is scheduled each day in the warm months (800/582-5956).

Dubuque Greyhound Park & Casino—The track, located on a river island at the base of the bridge linking Iowa to Wisconsin, features live greyhound racing May through October (800/373-3647).

Spirit of Dubuque— A cheery-looking yellow-and-white paddle wheeler is the place for family fun during the craft's narrated lunch, dinner, sightseeing and special-event cruises (800/747-8093).

Five Flags Theater (319/589-4254) and the Grand Opera House (319/588-1305)—Sister theaters downtown, both offer community and professional theater. Restored to its ornate splendor, Five Flags has box seats with plush scarlet cushions in the balcony that will take you back to the days of Sarah Bernhardt.

The Mathias Ham House—Set at the base of Eagle Point Park, this is Dubuque's only historic house museum. Opulent furnishings were shipped to the booming river town by steamboat from New Orleans and St. Louis in pre-Civil War times (800/226-3369).

SHOPPING

Cable Car Square— At the base of Dubuque's cable car track is a historic district with specialty and antiques shops and horse-drawn carriage rides (319/583-5000).

Harbor Place Mall— Housed in a restored factory along the

riverfront near the Mississippi River Museum, it offers booths with art, crafts and collectibles, as well as a large antique store (319/582-9227).

Farmers Market—The burnt orange of dried flower arrangements in the fall and the pale yellow of sweet corn in the summer brighten this open-air market Saturday mornings May through October (319/588-4400).

OUTDOOR RECREATION

Heritage Trail—Hikers, cyclists, photographers and fossil hunters take

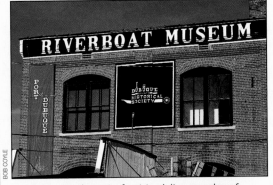

Head down to the waterfront to visit a complex of museums that includes one dedicated to river craft.

this 26-mile trail through woodlands, past railroad artifacts and rock outcroppings, and alongside friendly small towns (319/556-6745).

Mines of Spain Recreation Area—A National Historic Landmark, the 1,380-acre park contains nature trails and a limestone quarry, plus access to

the river through Catfish Creek for fishing and canoeing (319/556-0620).

Sundown Mountain Ski Area—The ski and snowboard park, five chairlifts and 22 runs up to 4,000 feet long—one with a 475-foot drop—draw crowds to slopes that cut through a century-old cedar forest (888/SUNDOWN).

Dubuque Yacht Basin RV Park—You can't get much closer to the river than this yacht basin, which offers camping, a boat launch, marina and 56 campsites (48 with electricity and water, 8 with full hook-up).

Visitors can bike or hike on the nearby flood wall that saved Dubuque from disaster during the Flood of '93 (319/556-7708).

Dubuque Arboretum & Botanical Gardens—Free Sunday evening concerts by local and regional performers throughout the summer draw picnickers to the arboretum, which is

supported by volunteer workers and boasts one of the largest public hosta gardens in the U.S., with some 13,000 plants of more than 900 varieties (319/556-2100).

FESTIVALS

Dubuquefest/Very Special Arts—Annually ushering in spring, the mid-May festival includes a big arts-and-crafts show in Washington Park, live music, food booths, a tour of Dubuque's grand old private homes and cultural events.

Dragon Boat Festival—Contestants from all over the world compete in mid-September races aboard the fearsome-looking brightly painted, 44-foot-long wooden boats that are much photographed and filmed by the national media.

Cable Car Square Chili Cook-Off and Fall Open House—Cornucopias on the stoops of the square's shops spill out fall's flaming palette of bittersweet and Indian corn during this salute to autumn in early October. (Call 800/798-8844 for a festival brochure.)

ALSO ALONG THE RIVER ROAD
Balltown

The pride and joy of Balltown (population: 100) is a hillcrest view of the surrounding emerald fields that reminds international travelers of Ireland. Locals claim that on a clear day you can see, if not quite forever, at least for 75 miles.

DINING

Breitbach's Country Dining—This family-run, meat-and-potatoes restaurant claims to be not only Iowa's oldest bar and restaurant, but also is the only one to have served the outlaw James brothers and the actress Brooke Shields (319/552-2220).

St. Donatus

An Old World village to the south of Dubuque, St. Donatus is known for the distinctive architecture of the homes built by immigrants from Luxembourg who used their native traditions to craft the stone walls of their low, eaveless homes, then coated them with stucco.

LODGINGS

Gehlen House B & B and Antiques—A hybrid of a bed and breakfast and antiques shop in an 1848 building listed in the National Register of Historic Places, it has seven rooms, including four suites with private baths. Doubles from $46 (319/773-8200).

DINING

Kalmes Store— Don't be put off by the modest exterior, which resembles a gas station and convenience store; the casual dining room inside serves wonderful Luxembourg specialties (319/773-2480).

SIGHTSEEING

Silent and otherworldly, the stations of the Outdoor Way of the Cross at the St. Donatus Catholic Church dot a steep hillside, offering both spiritual and physical exercise. Perched at the top is a small white chapel with a view of the surrounding valley.

Bellevue

Appropriately named in French for its "beautiful view," the little town of Bellevue (population: 2,500) has a layout that is simple and dramatic. It nestles between two wooded bluffs. Contact: Chamber of Commerce (319/872-5830).

LODGINGS

Spring Side Inn—This bed and breakfast, a rare Midwestern example

Punctuate a busy vacation schedule with a stop to admire the simple and serene architecture that adorns the hillside at St. Donatus, south of Dubuque.

of mid-19th century Gothic Revival architecture, serves a candlelight evening dessert. The six rooms are named for American authors—it seems only fitting that the Mark Twain room has an unsurpassed river view. Doubles from $120 (319/872-5452).

DINING

Riverview Cafe—Strangers are treated with both curiosity and hospitality in the old dining room of a downtown hotel, a favorite with locals for its homestyle food, including excellent pies and soups (319/872-4142).

OUTDOOR RECREATION

Bellevue State Park sits atop a bluff from which you can watch activity at the lock and dam in the pretty little town below. It also includes nature trails, 48 campsites (23 electric and 25 primitive) and a butterfly garden tended by locals (319/872-4019).

ACROSS THE RIVER SIGHTSEEING

In Dickeyville, Wisconsin, the stone shrines of the fanciful Dickeyville Grotto on the grounds of the Holy Ghost Parish have an offbeat charm. A parish priest built them in the 1920s using whatever was at hand,

including gearshift knobs from cars and pieces of crockery (608/568-3119).

FAMILY FUN
Dyersville

Founded in 1848, this pleasant little farm community of 3,800 is a half-hour west of Dubuque. Dyersville is known as the "Farm Toy Capital of the World" because of the trio of toy manufacturers here. Contact: Chamber of Commerce (319/875-2311).

DINING

In a setting of country antiques and vintage farm equipment, the cheery Country Junction restaurant serves the kind of homemade food that would have been served on the threshing tables of yesteryear (319/875-7055).

SIGHTSEEING

See miniature tractors and tiny combines during a tour of the Ertl Co., one of the country's largest manufacturers of toy farm equipment (319/875-5699). National Farm Toy Museum—"This is just like the one Dad had!" Visitors often exclaim this at the museum's displays of 30,000 replicated farm vehicles, from horse-drawn to contemporary. Dioramas honor the country's

agricultural heritage (319/875-2727). St Francis Xavier Basilica—The only U.S. basilica outside a metropolitan area, this Gothic structure looms up incongruously but strikingly on the surrounding landscape of cornfields. Inside it displays fine paintings; the light glows softly through the filter of its stained-glass windows (319/875-7325). *Field of Dreams* Movie Site—The tremendously popular and bittersweet movie about men, their fathers and baseball has prompted many to make pilgrimages to the place where it was filmed, a baseball diamond in the middle of a cornfield 3½ miles northeast of Dyersville (800/443-8981; 888/815-8404).

FESTIVALS

Largest Farm Toy Shows in the World—Aficionados from all over come to these shows the first full weekends in June and November (319/875-2727). The Festival of Arts—Held in late September in Dyersville. Talented crafters from around the Midwest sell their hand-produced wares at this popular festival. Highlights include a judged quilt show (319/875-2311).

By Rebecca Christian

GALENA

A picture-book Illinois town entices visitors with antiques shops, restaurants and inns.

Decades before the Gold Rush of 1849 saw California overrun with miners, northwestern Illinois had a mineral rush of its own. Fortune seekers from the South paddled up the Mississippi, and Yankee adventurers rode cross-country to converge in the town that took its name from the Latin word for lead, Galena. Built among the remote valleys and rolling hills of Jo Daviess County, Galena sat on top of one of the richest deposits of lead ore ever found.

Today, the pretty little hillside town (population: 3,647) is both an outdoor museum of Civil War-era architecture and a mecca for antiques lovers and history buffs. Back in the mid-1800s, Galena was the largest Mississippi River port north of St. Louis and the source of 80 percent of all of the lead mined in the world. Showy brick and stone mansions dotted its bluffs, and prosperous banks, dry goods stores and liveries lined its downtown streets.

Progress and history combined to change the course of Galena's fortunes. Railroads replaced steamboats. Erosion from careless mining and farming choked the Galena River with silt. Although the demand for ammunition briefly revived the town's lead trade during the Civil War, its hopes for a return to former prosperity died with the war's end.

Past Glories Renewed

In the long run, the downturn in prosperity became a boon for the town. Commercial decline left untouched a rich legacy of old buildings in Greek Revival, Queen Anne, Italianate, Second Empire, Romanesque Revival and Federal styles to be admired and restored in the 1960s. Today, 85 percent of Galena is listed as a National Register Historic District. The district embraces the long, narrow, curving main street of shops and residential streets where grand homes perch on terraced hills. Local ordinances control signage, design and renovation to help preserve the town's character and Civil War-era look. (The nostalgic scene in the movie *Field of Dreams*, in which Burt Lancaster's character returns to the town where he worked as a doctor, was filmed in Galena.)

Galena is home to a number of nationally known artists and craftspeople whose elegant galleries, working studios and upscale boutiques lend an

BOB COYLE

Historic buildings on the bluff above Galena's downtown.

unexpected city-style sophistication to this friendly, small town. Many Chicagoans escape the Windy City, driving 3 hours or so west to Galena for weekend getaways or to relax in the second homes they've renovated here.

No fewer than nine Civil War generals have lived here, the best known of whom was Ulysses S. Grant. On his triumphal return from the war in 1865, Galena's citizens presented Grant and his wife with a sturdy but modest brick home across the river from downtown. It's now the Ulysses S. Grant Home State Historic Site, restored to period decor using engravings from Grant's 1868 presidential campaign.

Getting to Know Galena

You'll receive an overview of Galena's charm on a self-guided walking tour of historic Main and Bench streets. Stop by the visitors center for a map. To explore the surrounding countryside, take the Stagecoach Trail between Galena and Lena. It follows an 1830s stagecoach route. Stop off for a sip of wine and a panoramic country view from the wraparound deck of Galena Cellars Vineyard Tasting Room.

In town, the Old Market House State Historic Site a block from Main Street features a short audiovisual show about the town's architecture. Its grounds are the site of an open-air market Saturday mornings in summer and fall. Visitors don hard hats for a trek through Vinegar Hill Historic Lead Mine & Museum, run by descendants of the Irishman who established the mine in 1822. The tour includes a walk down into the mine.

Galena visitors have been known to bypass the history lessons and head directly for the shops. During peak tourist season, parking along Main Street is at a premium, and tourists, nibbling fudge and other treats, throng the sidewalks. Coffee shops and casual eateries are tucked among gift shops, galleries and antiques emporiums.

Midwest Living readers voted Galena their "choice antiquing town" in 1992 and 1994. Shops feature refinished and as-found golden oak, Victorian and country furniture, along with pottery, lamps, linens and more. At Main Street Fine Books & Manuscripts, bibliophiles and students of history can lose whole afternoons searching among more than 30,000 out-of-print, antiquarian and first editions. Red's Antiques, Wholesale Barn & Auction House Service fills a barn with farm primitives and

Bakeries, boutiques and bistros line Galena's curving Main Street.

BOB COYLE

Bouncing along the old Stagecoach Trail.

machinery from weather vanes to well pumps, along with less easily identified items that prompt browsers to ask, "What do you think this was used for?"

Galena is a mother lode of interesting and varied accommodations. The town welcomes visitors with hotels, guest houses, bed and breakfasts, and inns. The 1855 DeSoto House Hotel in the heart of the historic district has an adjoining parking ramp and an imposing staircase popular for photo opportunities.

Away from the town center, you'll find condos, cabins and apartments that cater to couples and families vacationing together or holding family reunions. Eagle Ridge Inn & Resort, a complex set on thousands of densely wooded acres, has rooms, villas and homes for rent. Active vacationers like its cross-country ski trails, riding stable and three championship 18-hole golf courses.

Drive through the countryside around Galena and you'll be treated to hill-and-valley vistas that encompass lush farmlands, apple orchards and wineries. Some of the prettiest scenery is along these routes: Stagecoach Trail between Galena and Lena; Blackjack Road between Galena and Hanover; Derinda Road between Elizabeth and Mount Carroll; Canyon Park Road between Stockton and Warren; and the Great River Road passing through Galena and Hanover, tracing the mighty Mississippi on its way south.

TRAVEL GUIDE

Planning Your Visit to Galena

You'll find visitors centers in the old train depot two blocks north of US - 20 and at Market House Information Center, one block east of Main St. downtown. For information, contact: Galena/ Jo Daviess County Convention & Visitors Bureau (800/747-9377).

LODGINGS

Reservations are necessary for weekends, which usually require a 2-night minimum stay. Rates are lower midweek and off-season, November through March. The Convention & Visitors Bureau can provide a list of vacation rental agents who book privately owned homes, condos, cottages, cabins, and other types of accommodations (800/747-9377).

DeSoto House Hotel— Listed in the National Register of Historic Places, this downtown hotel boasts period decor, restaurants and retail shops. Doubles from $70 (800/343-6562).

Best Western Quiet House Suites—This modern motel ½ mile from downtown offers oversize rooms, suites with fireplaces, an indoor-outdoor pool and rooms decorated with themes such as Vintage Cabin and Mississippi

Riverboat. Doubles from $91 (800/528-1234).

Farmers' Guest House— Within walking distance of downtown, this restored 1867 guest house provides a hearty breakfast and several packages, including a history tour. Doubles from $79 (815/777-3456).

Renaissance Riverboat Suites & Rooms—Guest rooms, an apartment and luxury suites occupy two 1850s brick buildings within walking distance of downtown. All have access to an outdoor hot tub in a hillside cavern. Doubles from $75 (815/777-0123).

Eagle Ridge Inn & Resort—Surrounded by 6,800 wooded acres, this contemporary complex with country decor includes 80 rooms and 350 housing units, including one-, two- and three-bedroom villas and three-, four- and five-bedroom homes. Restaurants, indoor pool, fitness center, hiking trails, riding stable, tennis courts, four golf courses, cross-country ski trails, a sledding hill and an outdoor ice rink are among the amenities. Doubles from $120 (800/892-2269).

CAMPING

Palace Campground—A full-service campground with pool, hayrides, miniature golf and fishing is found on Galena's

west edge. It has 35 acres of tent camping and 105 RV spots. Reservations are recommended (815/777-2466).

DINING

Eldorado Grill— Acclaimed by food critics, this contemporary restaurant in the heart of the historic district specializes in naturally raised meats and produce, fresh fish, wild game and vegetarian dishes. Reservations are recommended (815/777-1224).

Cannova's Pizzeria— At this pleasant bistro downtown, the large pizza with imaginative toppings plus house salad make a perfect meal for two (815/777-3735).

Bubba's Seafood, Pasta & Smokehouse—Drop by this downtown spot for Cajun chicken, hickory-smoked ribs and fresh seafood— live Maine lobster, salmon, tuna and swordfish. Reservations are recommended (815/777-8030).

Cafe Italia—Grandma's pasta recipes prevail at this unpretentious Italian eatery downtown (815/777-0033).

Fried Green Tomatoes— This upscale Italian restaurant in a historic brick farmstead serves Black Angus steaks, fresh seafood and fried green tomatoes. Listen to piano bar enter-

tainment on Saturdays. Reservations are recommended (815/777-3938).
Vinny Vanucchi's—On the courtyard level of a historic building along Main St., this neighborhood Italian restaurant is one of the few eateries in the area with an outdoor cafe (815/777-8100).

SIGHTSEEING & ENTERTAINMENT

Galena/Jo Daviess County History Museum—Get acquainted with the area with the hourly audio-

Galena's Main Street meanders for several blocks, with tempting shops and eateries all along the way.

BOB COYLE

visual show in this 1858 Italianate mansion with exhibits about the Mississippi River and the Civil War (815/777-9129).
Ulysses S. Grant Home State Historic Site— Costumed interpreters at the 1860s home point out original furnishings and Grant's possessions. The gaslight tour at Christmas is a real treat (815/777-3310).
Old Market House State

Historic Site—A major renovation has spiffed up this 150-year-old Greek Revival building, the community's center during the halcyon days of antebellum prosperity (815/777-3310).
Vinegar Hill Historic Lead Mine & Museum— Learn about the lead that made Galena famous during this tour. Note: The mine is cramped, preventing adults from standing at full height (815/777-0855).
Galena Trolley Depot Tours—One-hour narrated trolley tours begin on the hour from 10 a.m. each day year-around (815/777-1248).
Galena Trolley Depot Theatre—Jim Post, Galena resident and Rock and Roll Hall of Fame inductee, performs one-man shows, including *Mark Twain and the Laughing River* (815/777-1248).
Galena Cellars Vineyard Tasting Room—Tour the bottling area of this country winery; then take in the view from its wraparound deck (815/777-3330).

ANTIQUING

Jo Daviess County is famous for antiques, with shops in even the smallest towns. Consult local newspapers for locations and listings of auctions in the area.
Red's Antiques, Whole-sale Barn & Auction House Service— Auctions take place most Saturday nights and flea markets every weekend from May to November. Farm primitives, furniture and machinery fill the big red barn. A lunch stand operates on auction days (815/777-9675).
Galena Antique Mall— Fifty dealers display their wares in this modern mall along US-20 (815/777-3440).

SHOPPING

Richard's New Antiques— This upscale shop has polished reproductions of 18th- and 19th-century English and French furniture, as well as bronzes, chandeliers and Tiffany-style lamps (815/777-1060).
Lloyd George— A dramatic skylight illuminates three floors of imports connected by a winding staircase: architectural fragments, South American folk

art, furniture, paintings and prints. A stone patio is the backdrop for garden furniture and statuary (815/777-3340).

The Toy Soldier Collection—Owner W. Paul LeGreco, dressed as Ulysses S. Grant, poses for pictures and makes hand-painted pewter figurines amid one of the largest collections of toy soldiers and military miniatures in North America (815/777-0383).

Follies—Unusual and whimsical crafts, gifts and jewelry include the collectible Christmas ornaments of Christopher Radko and Dresden Dove (815/777-1477).

Main Street Fine Books & Manuscripts—You'll find autographs, historic documents and first editions at this nationally known shop (815/777-3749).

Carl Johnson Gallery—Original watercolors painted by the owner on location in Galena, Chicago, the U.S. and Europe are on display (815/777-1222).

Leslie Howard Gallery—Fabergé eggs, nesting dolls and colorful lacquered boxes lend an exotic touch to this shop that specializes in handcrafted folk art and decorative accessories from Russia and Europe (815/777-8033).

OUTDOOR RECREATION

Galena Mountain Bike Rental—Explore the challenging roads surrounding Galena on mountain bikes. This rental is found just inside the floodgates downtown (815/777-3409).

Chestnut Mountain Resort—Winter fun at this blufftop resort with 120 rooms includes downhill skiing with 19 runs, snowboarding and an alpine slide on which a wheeled sled descends a bluff for 2,500 feet to the

Look up! Galena's rich legacy of 19th-century buildings means there's always something to see.

Mississippi River (800/397-1320).

Shenandoah Riding Center—One-hour guided trail rides are available year-round at this stable, 6 miles east of Galena. Hayrides and sleighrides can be arranged in season (815/777-2373).

FESTIVALS

Tour of Historic Homes—This popular mid-June event, a tradition since the 1940s, combines tours of homes, notable gardens and the county historical museum (815/777-9129).

Galena Arts Festival—An annual crowd-pleaser in late July features more than 100 booths of juried fine arts, live music and food (815/777-1948).

OTHER PLACES TO VISIT

LODGINGS

The Farm—A converted barn and chicken coop house hot tubs and fireplaces at a bed and breakfast in a secluded country setting near Mt. Carroll, 45 minutes southeast of Galena (815/244-9885).

DINING

Mulgrew's Tavern and Liquor Store—This all-American down-home tavern in East Dubuque, 10 miles west of Galena, has a collection of caps embellished with witty sayings behind the bar and specializes in chili dogs (815/747-8861).

Timmerman's Supper Club—A longtime local favorite in East Dubuque, this blufftop restaurant looks across the Mississippi to Iowa. Famous for Sunday brunch, all-you-can-eat shrimp on Fridays, and homemade banana bread (815/747-3316).

SIGHTSEEING & SHOPPING

Scales Mound—All of this 1855 town of 388 just north of the Stagecoach Trail is listed in the National Register of Historic Places. The charming Scales Mound City Park has an original band-stand and town hall.

Kolb-Lena Cheese Company—East of Lena along US-20, visitors to this outlet store can sample specialty cheeses—Camembert, Brie, goat's milk with roasted garlic and the company's specialty, mild Baby Swiss (815/369-4577).

Blue Hollow Farm—Dried flowers, herb teas and herb honeys, dried herbs and spices, and some 500 varieties of live herb plants line the shelves of this pungent nursery and shop on an old farm in Stockton (population: 1,871), east of Galena (815/947-2448).

The Pulford Opera House Antique Mall—In the Mississippi River town of Savanna, 25 miles south of Galena, this turn-of-the-century building houses more than 100 dealers (815/273-2661).

Whistling Wings, Inc.—In Hanover (population: 908), the "Mallard Capital of the World" raises 200,000 birds a year. At the hatchery downtown, you can watch an instructional videotape, see baby ducks and buy products such as smoked mallard and duck sausage. In late September, the town celebrates Mallardfest with a parade, duck-calling contest and Apple River Duck Race (815/591-3512).

OUTDOOR RECREATION

Apple River Canyon State Park—The Apple River flows through the canyons of this popular state park between Stockton and Warren. Along with hiking trails, there is camping April 15 through October at 50 sites (815/745-3302).

Mississippi Palisades State Park—Thirty miles south of Galena along US-20 and State-84 in Savanna, the park offers camping, hiking and rock climbing along the sheer cliffs and deep ravines of the Upper Mississippi

Civil War General and U.S. President Ulysses S. Grant is Galena's hometown hero.

(815/273-2731).

Long Hollow Tower & Scenic Overlook—Climb the lookout tower between Galena and Elizabeth along US-20 for a spectacular view of Jo Daviess County's rugged valleys and rolling hills.

Brookside Trout Fishery—April through November, learn about fly fishing and try catch-and-release stream fishing at this spring-fed waterway between Lake Galena and Apple Canyon Lake (815/845-2251).

Frentress Lake Marine Center—Use the slip rental, dock, showers and other amenities at this marina east of the East Dubuque bridge (815/747-3155).

FESTIVALS

Stagecoach Trail Festival—Stagecoach rides and a reenactment of a stagecoach robbery are highlights of this late June festival that takes place in the small towns of Lena, Nora, Warren, Apple River, Scales Mound and Galena all linked by the Stagecoach Trail (800/747-9377).

Klondike Kapers and Winter Carnival—Held at Chestnut Mountain Resort, events in late January and late February feature skydivers, snow sculptures, barbecue on the slopes and fireworks (815/777-1320).

By Rebecca Christian

65

THE
QUAD CITIES

**Crisscross the Mississippi
to experience the myriad of
sights and attractions in this
quartet of cities.**

A charming Native American legend holds that the Mississippi, making its initial journey southward to the sea, saw land so enchanting it turned for a longer look and forever changed course. The Quad Cities of Davenport and Bettendorf, Iowa, and Rock Island and Moline, Illinois, cluster at that point, one of the few places where the river runs east to west. The two-way flow of the river makes giving directions a challenge; most locals use "left" and "right" rather than "east" and "west" when helping to orient visitors.

Midway between Chicago (160 miles to the east) and Des Moines (175 miles west), the Quad Cities have a combined population of 400,000, making them the second-largest metropolitan area in Iowa. With museums, Civil War-era sites, music festivals and riverboat gambling, they're a lively destination for a weekend getaway or mini-vacation.

The Mississippi River is both the commercial heart of the two-state region and its principal attraction, alternately bustling and serene as it winds through the Quad Cities. Unlike river towns in which water vistas are hidden away behind high levees, much of the riverfront here is open, drawing visitors with panoramic views and miles of hiking and bicycling trails along the water.

Trains, Tractors
And Troops

Over the years, Davenport, the largest of the Quad Cities, has been a fur-trading settlement, a War of 1812 battleground and a center for steamboating, railroading, and manufacturing of farm implements. As a young attorney, Abraham Lincoln argued for the rights of the upstart railroad industry against the powerful steamboat interests.

Lincoln's side won, and railroads spanning the river began to ship wares from local manufacturers such as farm-machinery giant John Deere & Co. The company remains a big presence in town. Its logo—a leaping deer on a bright green background—marks the John Deere Pavilion, a

RUSS MUNN

$7 million complex in downtown Moline, in a parklike setting near the river. Kids will marvel at vintage and up-to-date farm machinery, and have fun interacting with state-of-the-art exhibits that trace the role of agriculture from the moment the seed is planted in the field until the cook puts the food on the table.

Head to 3-mile-long Arsenal Island, the largest island in the Upper Mississippi, for a geographical and historical overview of the area. Steeped in Civil War history, the island is where the fictional Ashley Wilkes languished in a Yankee prison in *Gone with the Wind* and where 2,000 Confederate soldiers are, in fact, buried. The cemetery's somber rows of headstones make poignant reminders of the Midwest's involvement in the War Between the States.

Established in 1862, the arsenal supplied the Union Army and still serves as the headquarters for the U.S. Army's Industrial Operations Command.

The complex's massive limestone buildings include a museum displaying munitions from the Battle of Little Bighorn to Desert Storm. Also on its grounds is the 1833 Federal-style home of the founder of Davenport, Colonel George Davenport. The Mississippi River visitors center here overlooks the site where Lock and Dam No. 15 tames the once-treacherous Rock Island Rapids.

Fun Times Four

In the arsenal neighborhood, you'll find the Arts and Entertainment District, an area of brew pubs, nightlife and galleries along the river in downtown Rock Island. Three floating casinos and a 400-passenger non-gaming boat dock nearby.

Riverbend Antiques, along the riverfront in Davenport, is a high-quality antiques store in an intriguing labyrinth of Civil War-era red brick buildings linked by a central courtyard. Occasionally tourists spot celebrity customers browsing among the Art Deco chandeliers, vintage linens, stoneware pottery and antique toys.

Shopping is a prime attraction across the river at the Village of East

Bettendorf's Abbey Hotel was the home of cloistered nuns.

RUSS MUNN

Jazz lovers honor Bix Beiderbecke in Davenport.

Davenport, a 120-acre historic district with more than 500 homes and businesses. Homes that date to the 1830s sit amid gardens growing bright, old-fashioned flowers such as sunflowers and sweet Williams. Along East 11th and 12th streets are six square blocks of art galleries, specialty shops, antiques shops and restaurants to explore. Stop by Isabel Bloom to see the hand-finished work of this regionally famous local sculptor.

Not far away is blufftop Lindsay Park, once a training ground for Union Soldiers. Now, this leafy site provides fine views of the Mississippi River and Arsenal Island.

Two Davenport museums sit side by side on Museum Hill. The Putnam Museum of History and Natural Science is a hands-on facility with fox pelts to stroke and a steamboat wheel to turn. The Davenport Museum of Art is known for its collection of Midwest regional art and Grant Wood memorabilia.

The area's 50 miles of off-street hiking and biking trails include the Great River Trail, which begins at Credit Island in west Davenport and seldom loses sight of the river. Linked to the Great River Trail is one that

leads to Sylvan Island. Despite its location in the middle of a metropolitan area in Moline, Sylvan Island serves as a habitat for beavers, eagles, muskrats, squirrels and birds. Recent improvements include walkways, new fishing piers and the restoration of a footbridge more than a century old.

Traveling on the *Channel Cat Water Taxi*, also in Moline, is a fun way to explore the Quad Cities. This pontoon boat makes hour-long loops across the river between Moline, Bettendorf and the Village of East Davenport. Cyclists can bring their bikes onboard, hopping on and off to see the sights and to try out trails on both sides of the river.

On the last full weekend in July, the Quad Cities are a prime destination for jazz fans and runners. The area's biggest summer festival is named after legendary trumpeter and native son Bix Beiderbecke. Staged outdoors in Davenport's riverfront LeClaire Park, The Bix Beiderbecke Memorial Jazz Festival showcases a dozen local and national jazz ensembles. On Saturday morning, the city blooms with color and motion as 20,000 runners and walkers sweep through the streets of Davenport in a 7-mile run.

Planning Your Visit to the Quad Cities

For information, contact: Quad Cities Convention & Visitors Bureau (800/747-7800; http:// quadcities.com/cvb).

LODGINGS

Chain motels cluster along I-80, downtown, I-74 and the airport corridor. Abbey Hotel—This elegant, European-style, 19-room hotel in Bettendorf was once a peaceful cloister for Carmelite nuns. Built in 1916, the buff-colored brick former monastery welcomes visitors with stained-glass windows, a sprawling garden courtyard and an outdoor swimming pool. Doubles from $75 (800/438-7535). The Blackhawk Hotel— This renovated 1914 hotel stands along the riverfront in Davenport two blocks from the *President Riverboat Casino.* It features a sports bar and grill, a steak house, modern rooms and an exercise/workout room. Doubles from $59 (800/553-1173). Jumer's Castle Lodge— This nine-story local landmark and award- winning hotel in Bettendorf has a Bavarian atmosphere, along with 210 rooms, German food and indoor pool. Doubles from $87

(800/285-8637). Fulton's Landing—This newly renovated bed and breakfast in an 1871 home on Davenport's majestic E. River Dr. was voted the area's "friendliest bed and breakfast." Bicycling and walking paths wind in front of the home, listed in the National Register of Historic Places. Doubles from $60 (800/397-4068). The Potter House— This romantic Rock Island bed and breakfast, listed in the National Register of Historic Places, is a restored 1907 home. A stay includes a full breakfast. Doubles from $75 (800/747-0339).

DINING

Lagomarcino's—This charming and authentic 1908 downtown Moline confectionery and ice cream store serves snacks and lunch amid cozy mahogany booths, Tiffany-style lamps and a tin ceiling. The rich ice cream and candy are made on the premises. An old-fashioned soda fountain serves phosphates and sodas (309/764-1814). Christie's—This gourmet restaurant with an imaginative menu and daily specials is located in a Victorian house in the village of East Davenport (319/323-2822). C'est Michele—This award-winning French restaurant in Moline is ideal for celebrating special occasions with a six-course fixed-price menu. Make reserva- tions well in advance (309/762-0585).

Old-fashioned treats draw visitors to Lagomarcino's, a vintage ice cream and candy shop in Moline, Illinois.

Thunder Bay Grille—Look for north-woods style decor and dining with steaks, chops, pasta and salads in Davenport (319/386-2722).

SIGHTSEEING & ENTERTAINMENT

The President Riverboat Casino—A soaring atrium and crystal chandeliers grace this 1936 National Historic Landmark along Davenport's riverfront. The casino has dockside gaming year-round and cruises from May through October (800/262-8711).

Jumer's Casino Rock Island—This floating complex includes a barge museum, a restaurant on a towboat and a paddlewheeler casino at The Boatworks on the Rock Island Riverfront (800/477-8946).

Lady Luck Casino—The newest of the Quad's three floating casinos, this Bettendorf attraction boasts 30,000 square feet of gaming space and a 70-item international buffet at lunch and dinner (800/724-5825).

Queen of Hearts—A 400-passenger non-gaming boat operated by Celebration River Cruises departs from the Moline riverfront for daily lunch, dinner and twilight cruises.

Reservations are recommended (800/297-0034).

John Deere Pavilion—This striking and contemporary exhibition hall with a gift shop tells the

Barges on the Mississippi River make their way through the lock and dam at Rock Island, Illinois.

story of the venerable Moline-based manufacturer of farm, construction, and lawn and garden equipment through an interactive display (309/765-1000).

Circa 21 Dinner Playhouse—The facility hosts a year-round professional dinner theater, concerts and improvisational comedy appropriate for families in a restored 1920s-era vaudeville house in Rock Island's Arts and Entertainment District (309/786-7733).

Rock Island Arsenal—A cross between a military post, small town and tourist attraction, this complex on a Mississippi River island is well worth a half day. Attractions include: Rock Island Arsenal Museum, with a

fascinating collection of weaponry (309/782-5021); the Mississippi River Visitors Center overlooking Lock and Dam No. 15 (309/794-5338); the restored Colonel George Davenport Home; the 4-mile long Rock Island Arsenal Bike Trail; National Cemetery; and Confederate Cemetery, where the Southern soldiers who died in the island's prisoner of war camp during the Civil War are laid to rest. Access the island from Government Bridge, one of the few remaining swing bridges operating on the river.

Museum Hill—Lifelike dioramas and artifacts tell the story of the river and the region. Kids love the Hall of Mammals at Putnam Museum of History and Natural Science (319/324-1933). Next door, the Davenport Museum of Art features a collection of Midwest art, along with memorabilia of the

Heartland artist in overalls, Grant Wood, who painted the classic *American Gothic*. The museum has a special just-for-kids section, where youngsters can explore art in new ways (319/326-7804).

Family Museum of Arts & Science—New in Bettendorf, this is part of The Learning Campus, a $12 million project that combines a library, children's museum and cultural arts center into a single facility. The museum includes exhibits on the science and art of sound and music, and on farming and weather (319/344-4106).

Quad City River Bandits—Watch the Houston Astros' Class-A farm team at John O'Donnell Stadium along Davenport's lively riverfront (319/324-2032).

SHOPPING

Retail Malls—NorthPark in Davenport, Iowa's largest retail mall, features a mini roller coaster and carousel (319/391-4500). SouthPark in Moline holds the bragging rights as the biggest mall in downstate Illinois (309/797-9070).

Antique American Mall— Just off I-80, this 110-dealer mall is a great resource for serious antiques collectors (319/386-3430).

Riverbend Antiques— A half-block of antiques and collectibles near the river in Davenport, this shop is a favorite stop for celebrities performing in town and for film makers who are decorating sets (319/323-8622).

Trash Can Annie—Next door to Riverbend Antiques sits one of the country's largest vintage clothing stores. The 50,000-item inventory includes garments and accessories from pioneer days to the heyday of the '70s disco craze (319/322-5893).

Village of East Davenport—Lush gardens and some of the area's oldest homes enrich this historic shopping and strolling

district. Browse through more than 50 galleries, restaurants and specialty shops (319/322-0546).

OUTDOOR RECREATION

Sylvan Island—Shaded by cottonwoods and silver maples, the 38-acre river island in Moline has been newly converted into a recreation area with paths and fishing piers (309/797-0785). A bicycle trail on the island connects to the

The historic Rock Island Arsenal complex includes two cemeteries, museums and a weapons plant.

Great River Trail. In Iowa, the trail starts at Credit Island in west Davenport and for 6 miles keeps the river almost always in sight. The Great River Trail in Illinois is part of a more than 60-mile trail that stretches from Rock Island to Savanna, Illinois.

Hennepin Canal Parkway—Part of a 70-mile "greenway" that runs from the Quad Cities to LaSalle-Peru, Illinois, a 5-mile paved portion crosses south Rock Island and Milan.

Duck Creek Parkway—This stretch of green winds along its namesake creek for 13 miles through Davenport and Bettendorf. Contact: Quad Cities Convention & Visitors Bureau (800/747-7800).

EMPIRE (East Moline Playground Innovation Recreation Efforts)—Children love the swings and mazes of this 14,000-square-foot playground funded by donations and built by volunteers on Illinois-84 along the East Moline/Hampton border.

Lindsay Park—Located near the Village of East Davenport on the site of Camp McLellan, a training post for Iowa and Illinois soldiers during the Civil War, the park offers views of the river and Rock Island Arsenal.

Vander Veer Park Botanical Center—Unlike many conservatories, the greenhouse area that grows the plants and flowers is open to the public. The rose garden is considered one of the Midwest's finest (319/326-7818).

FESTIVALS

Bix Beiderbecke Memorial Jazz Festival—This nationally known event pays tribute to native son Beiderbecke with 3 days of music, arts-and-crafts fairs and a road race the last full weekend in July (319/324-7170).

Quad City Air Show—This 2-day "festival in the sky" draws thousands in June to the Davenport Municipal Airport with daredevil acrobatics, skydivers and vintage aircraft that re-create famous air battles (319/322-7469).

Quad Cities Classic PGA Tour—Top professional golfers compete for a $1 million total purse during the second week of July in nearby Coal Valley, Illinois. The tour also features food vendors, events and entertainment (800/336-4655).

Beaux Arts Festival—This twice-yearly event features more than 100 juried artists on the grounds of the Davenport Museum of Art. The festival is held on Mother's Day and on the weekend after Labor Day (319/326-7804).

Winter Events Bald Eagle Days—Guided eagle-watching trips, environmental exhibits and a wildlife art show are held in early January in the Quad Cities, a prime eagle-watching territory in winter (309/799-5912).

North of the Quad Cities
SIGHTSEEING

The Twilight—For an authentic adventure, take a two-day cruise aboard this Victorian-style steamboat. The boat cruises from LeClaire, Iowa, to Galena, Illinois, where guests stay overnight at a ski lodge and see the sights the next morning before returning to port (800/331-1467).

Cody Homestead—Tour the LeClaire, Iowa, boyhood home of the famous Wild West showman William F. (Buffalo Bill) Cody. The house was built of native limestone in the Wapsipinicon River Valley in 1847. It's furnished authentically in early 1900s style (319/225-2981).

Walnut Grove Pioneer Village—Five miles west of the Cody Homestead is this site of an early crossroads settlement. A bank, schoolhouse and blacksmith shop are among 18 old buildings that have been moved here and filled with artifacts (319/285-9903).

Scott County Park—This park includes 1,000 wooded acres with camping, hiking, equestrian trails and an Olympic-size pool (319/328-3280).

By Rebecca Christian

RIVERBOAT TERRITORY

Travel to the easy-going river towns of western Illinois and eastern Missouri, and you'll find yourself in familiar territory. Samuel Clemens, better known by the pen name Mark Twain, so brilliantly captured the Mississippi's riverboat era that you may feel as if you've been here before.

Twain's connection to the river was early and profound. In *Life on the Mississippi*, he reminisced about growing up in Hannibal, Missouri: "When I was a boy, there was but one permanent ambition among my comrades in our village on the west bank of the Mississippi River. That was, to be a steamboatman. . . ." The arrival of steamboats, one from St. Louis and another from Keokuk, Iowa, were the two great events in an otherwise dull day. Twain and his friends eagerly welcomed these marvelous craft on the river.

In every hamlet along the river, the cry "Steamboat a-comin'!" signaled townsfolk to hurry to the river. They watched as a marvel of technology, decorated with all the bric-a-brac of the Victorian age, churned toward them, with black smoke rolling from its stacks.

Twain did become a steamboatman. When he started writing, he adopted a most appropriate pseudonym from that first career: "Mark Twain!" was the call of the boat's leadsman as he plumbed the depth of the mighty river.

Twain's prose rendered vivid images of steamboats, from the elaborate chimneys and the pilot house made of glass and gingerbread trim to the flag that snapped in the breeze. Even today, readers easily can imagine furnace doors that opened to reveal the burning heart of the vessel,

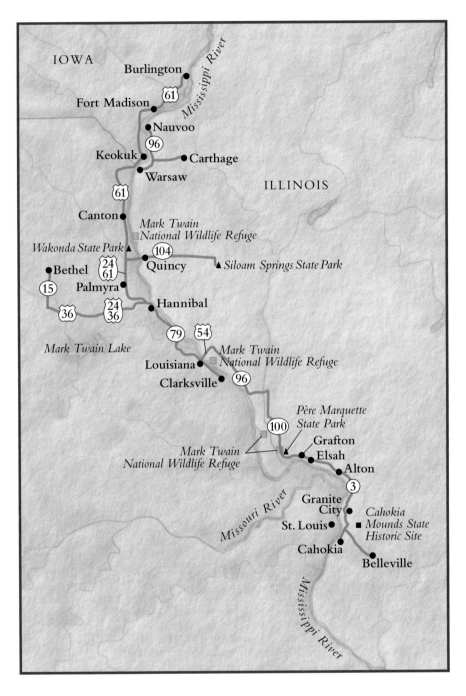

while passengers lined the upper deck, and the captain, the most imposing figure of all, rang the bell and commanded the paddle wheels to halt in the foamy water.

Fortunately, destinations along the Mississippi River still recall Twain's uniquely American vision.

NAUVOO

On a promontory overlooking the Mississippi, a tranquil village remembers its past.

Nauvoo, a small river town, nestles in a sweeping horseshoe bend of the Mississippi in western Illinois. Once the largest city in the state, it's now a quiet village, a center for the surrounding farming community. Nauvoo's early history, however, was not so peaceful.

Stronghold for a New Religion

The Mormon church (formally called the Church of Jesus Christ of Latter-day Saints) was less than a decade old in 1839 when Joseph Smith and his followers journeyed to Illinois to establish a settlement. The Mormons built their town on Mississippi River flats where Sac and Fox Indians once farmed. They called their settlement Nauvoo, which means "beautiful place" in Hebrew.

By 1844, Nauvoo had grown to become one of the 10 largest cities in the U.S., boasting hundreds of fine brick homes, two newspapers, a university and its own militia. Atop the hill overlooking the settlement loomed a large limestone temple, the center of Mormon life in Nauvoo.

Yet, for all their planning, the Mormons hadn't foreseen the resentment their prosperity and religion would stir among other settlers. In 1844, church leader Joseph Smith was assassinated. Two years later, the Mormons abandoned Nauvoo. Smith's successor, Brigham Young, led thousands of followers westward to the territory that became the state of Utah. Others relocated to Independence, Missouri.

Although Nauvoo never regained its early stature, it attracted settlers after the Mormon exodus. The French Icarians, a utopian community founded by Etienne Cabet, settled here shortly after the Mormons fled. Their experimental commune (in which members pursued "terrestrial paradise") collapsed a few years later amid internal rebellion.

German immigrants arrived next. They nurtured the vineyards planted by the Icarians, and wine making thrived. The newcomers built sturdy homes and shops on the hill above the original Mormon settlement, and the town assumed a new identity.

For many years, the red brick homes of Old Nauvoo slumbered on the river flats. Then, in the

JOHN TELFORD

PRINTIN

Costumed
interpreters in
Old Nauvoo.

1960s, Mormon descendants of Nauvoo's original settlers began returning to rebuild the abandoned structures. Today, many church members from around the country volunteer to work as guides, costumed in the calico dresses and homespun fashions of their ancestors.

Historic Sites

Old Nauvoo includes more than 20 restored structures. They line quiet leafy lanes near the marshy banks of the Mississippi. Visitors linger at two homes once occupied by Joseph Smith: an 1803 log cabin, which is the town's oldest structure and Smith's first home here, and a refined Federal-style clapboard house which Smith owned just before his death. Fascinating artifacts dating to the 1840s fill the town's original post office, meeting house, gunsmithing shop and newspaper office.

At the village blacksmith, a burly artisan explains how the Mormons made thousands of wagons in just a few short months in 1846 to prepare for the long trek to Utah. For a break, drop by the Scovil Bakery for tempting cookies still warm from the oven. Then you may want to board a horse-drawn carriage for a guided tour of the picturesque settlement. If you feel independent, strike out on your own and explore other buildings.

Up the hill lies another legacy of the Mormon era: the foundation of the magnificent temple that dominated the city before being destroyed by fire in 1848. The parklike surroundings include one of 30 "sunstones" that served as capitals on the temple columns, plus a small replica of the original temple.

Modern Nauvoo

Modern Nauvoo adjoins the hilltop temple site. A small town of 1,100, it caters to visitors and area farmers. On the town's main thoroughfare, Mulholland Street, you'll find antiques shops and artisans. Don't pass up the

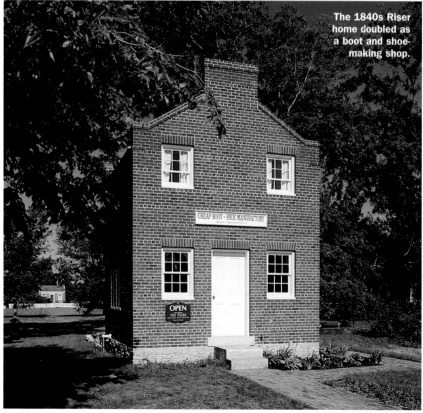

The 1840s Riser home doubled as a boot and shoe-making shop.

HISTORIC NAUVOO

Nauvoo celebrates its history as a wine and cheese center.

Nauvoo Mill & Bakery, where you can buy a loaf of freshly baked bread or a sack of flour for your own baking.

Nearby is the venerable Hotel Nauvoo, built in 1840. Stay overnight at the hotel or at least stop by to order some crunchy fried chicken, the specialty on the ample buffet menu.

You also can treat yourself to local wines and Nauvoo blue cheese, which the French Icarians introduced in the 19th century. These settlers discovered that Nauvoo's soil and climate were ideal for growing grapes. They planted vineyards on the surrounding hills. Although the Icarians' utopia failed rather quickly, their agricultural innovations endured. Vintners eventually honeycombed the region's bluffs with stone-lined wine cellars to store the fruit of their labors.

Although Prohibition, which was initiated in the 1920s, ended Nauvoo's thriving wine industry, the cool, moist cellars proved the ideal environment for another enterprise, cheese making. The area has produced famed Nauvoo blue cheese, a creamy and fragrant creation prized by cheese fanciers since the late 1930s.

One winery and several vineyards still continue the region's grape-growing traditions. Long rows of grapevines at the Baxter Winery and Vineyards (Illinois' oldest) adjoin Nauvoo State Park. In the tasting room, guests sip samples of Concord, the winery's sweet signature vintage.

Major Festivals

Each Labor Day weekend, the Nauvoo Grape Festival highlights the town's famous wine and cheese. Other planned holiday activities include road races, parades, as well as an arts-and-crafts festival.

Another popular event occurs in August, when more than 300 actors from around the country dramatize the Mormon saga in the *City of Joseph,* an outdoor musical that has won praise as one of the best outdoor pageants in the nation. Performed on an awesome five-level, 300-foot stage overlooking the river, the annual show celebrates the courage and determination of the early pioneers who first settled the Nauvoo area.

Today, the town testifies to the healing power of time. Home for only a few years to the early Mormons, Nauvoo attracts visitors of all faiths and nationalities. Strolling the communities' peaceful lanes and lingering along the scenic Mississippi River, visitors will agree that Nauvoo is indeed a "beautiful place" that has made peace with its turbulent past.

Planning Your Visit to Nauvoo

For information about Nauvoo, contact: Nauvoo Chamber of Commerce (217/453-6648). For information about Old Nauvoo, contact: L.D.S. Visitors Center (800/453-0022 or 217/453-2233). For general travel information, contact: Western Illinois Development Office (309/837-7460).

LODGINGS

Choose from bed and breakfasts, family-owned motels and campgrounds. The Hotel Nauvoo—Built as a home in 1840, this downtown Nauvoo inn has six rooms and two suites. Doubles from $48 (217/453-2211). The Ancient Pines Bed & Breakfast—Only several yards from the vineyards stands this turn-of-the-century home with stained-glass windows, pressed metal ceilings and herb and flower gardens. Three guest rooms share two baths. Doubles from $49 (217/453-2767). Mississippi Memories Bed & Breakfast—Just south of town, this multilevel home overlooking the Mississippi has four guest rooms. Breakfast on Belgian waffles that are served with fresh seasonal fruit. Doubles from $65 (217/453-2771).

DINING

Hotel Nauvoo—The hotel's restaurant is a local favorite for fried chicken (217/453-2211). Nauvoo Mill & Bakery—Long an establishment along Mulholland St., the bakery serves deli sandwiches made with stone-ground wheat breads, plus all kinds of homemade cookies (217/453-6734). Grandpa John's Cafe—Also along Mulholland St., this lunch spot is known for burgers, soda fountain treats and home-cooked fare (217/453-2310).

SIGHTSEEING

The Church of Jesus Christ of Latter-day Saints Visitors Center—At the northern edge of the historic site, see exhibits and a film about Nauvoo history. Outside, view 13 life-size statues in the Monument to Women Garden (800/453-0022). Joseph Smith Historic Center—On the southern edge of Old Nauvoo, see a presentation about local history and tour Smith's grave site and home (217/453-2246). Icarian Living History Museum—Learn about the utopian group's settlement in Nauvoo (217/453-2281).

RECREATION & ATTRACTIONS

Nauvoo State Park—This site, adjacent to Old Nauvoo, has 150 campsites, a 1½-mile hiking trail, and fishing and boating on 13-acre Lake Horton (217/453-2512). The Baxter Winery and Vineyards—Illinois' oldest winery dates from 1857. Enjoy wine tasting, a gift shop and tours (217/453-2528). Allyn House—Shop for a variety of Nauvoo-related gifts along Mulholland St. (217/453-2204). *City of Joseph*—The story of the Mormons in Nauvoo is a much-praised open-air theater event presented every August. The river serves as a magnificent backdrop (217/453-2237).

FESTIVALS

Labor Day weekend is the time to celebrate the area's wine heritage at The Nauvoo Grape Festival (217/453-6648).

OTHER PLACES TO VISIT IN THE AREA

Fort Madison, Iowa

Upriver from Nauvoo lies Fort Madison, site of the first U.S. Army fort west of the Mississippi. The mighty river widens into 30,000-acre Lake Cooper at this point, its broad channel spanned by the Santa Fe Railroad Bridge, the world's longest double-deck swinging bridge. In this city of 12,000, see nearly 100 Victorian homes, plus a reconstruction of the 1808 fort. To get there from Nauvoo, take State-96 north for 9 miles, then cross the river at Niota. For further information about this area, contact: Riverbend Regional Convention & Visitors Bureau (800/210-8687 or 319/372-5472).

LODGINGS

Kingsley Inn—This elegant inn overlooks the river just across from Riverview Park. Along with family-style dining at Alpha's Restaurant, there are 14 guest rooms and one suite. Doubles from $70 (800/441-2327).

At Fort Madison, Iowa, visit the first U.S. military outpost, now reconstructed, west of the Mississippi.

Kountry Klassic— Guests retire to sweet dreams and awaken with hearty appetites at this lodging—perhaps because of home-made chocolates tucked under their pillows and the farm-fresh eggs served at breakfast. This lodging has two rooms with private baths and two others with a shared

bath. Doubles from $75 (888/310-6549).

Morrison Manor— Victorian antiques and Oriental carpets embellish this 1881 home's four guest rooms, each with private bath. Doubles from $70 (319/372-5876).

SIGHTSEEING

Fort Madison recalls its heritage in a number of sites in Riverview Park along the Mississippi. Old Fort Madison is a replica of the fort that once guarded American interests on the frontier. (Indians sieged the original fort in 1813.

Then garrison troops set it afire before fleeing by boat downriver.) Guides wearing rough frontier homespun recall life in this isolated outpost (319/372-6318). Beside the fort is the North Lee County Historical Center housed in the town's former railroad station, which dates from the turn of

the century. Inside, learn about ice gathering on the Mississippi, frontier and railroad history, and the area's Native American heritage. Next door, the Flood Museum chronicles the great Mississippi River flood of 1993. Photos, newspaper clippings, and television footage help tell the story of one of the river's greatest disasters (319/372-7661). The Fort Madison Farmington & Western Railroad Museum—Hop aboard a turn-of-the-century train for a 2-mile ride. Then view antique locomotives and tour the old-fashioned depot. The museum is off State-2 between Fort Madison and Donnellson, Iowa (319/837-6689). The Catfish Bend Riverboat Casino—This 1,500-passenger riverboat, built in the style of a 19th-century sternwheeler, docks in Riverview Park from May through October. (In October, the boat heads to Burlington where it docks along the riverfront until May.) The boat cruises Mondays through Fridays (800/372-2946).

FESTIVALS

Old Fort Madison holds living history events year-round, including an 1813 muster in June, a military history weekend in July, a rodeo rendezvous in September and lovely candlelight tours in October. The Tri-State Rodeo, one of the region's largest, is held the weekend after Labor Day (319/372-2550).

Burlington, Iowa

Burlington perches on scenic bluffs overlooking the Mississippi. Founded in 1808, it became the first territorial capital of Iowa. Cliffs that once yielded flint for Indian arrows soon bustled with frontier homes and buildings. Today, Burlington is a city of 30,000, known for its famous Snake Alley, a winding street built to connect bluff-top homes with the downtown area along the river.

To reach Burlington from Nauvoo, take IL State-96 north to Fort Madison, then go north for 18 miles on US-61. For information, contact: Burlington Convention & Visitors Bureau (800/827-4837 or 319/752-6365).

LODGINGS

The Schramm House Bed & Breakfast—This 1870s Queen Anne home with four guest rooms boasts period antiques. French toast with caramelized apples and vegetable frittata are breakfast specialties. Doubles from $75 (319/754-0373). Mississippi Manor—

The 1877 Italianate structure, once home to a lumber baron, has two guest rooms, two suites and a studio apartment with cooking facilities. Doubles from $60 (319/753-2218).

DINING

Big Muddy's—This turn-of-the-century railroad freight station along the riverfront has been transformed into a casual restaurant. Amid railroad memorabilia, select from a varied menu featuring catfish, steak, pasta, soups and sandwiches (319/753-1699). The Jefferson Street Cafe—Housed in a historic downtown building on Jefferson St., this casual dining spot specializes in steaks and pasta (319/754-1036).

SIGHTSEEING

Port of Burlington Welcome Center—In a 1928 building along 400 N. Front St., where Mississippi barges were once loaded with coal, the center shows a video featuring local attractions and shares information about area history (319/752-8731). Snake Alley—Known as one of the most crooked streets in the world, the cobblestone lane zigzags precariously from the bluff to the downtown level (a drop of 58 feet). The Des Moines County Historical Society—This dedicated organization on Sixth St. runs three museums: Phelps House, an elegant Victorian mansion at the upper end of Snake Alley; the Hawkeye Log Cabin in Crapo Park, a frontier home with period

At the Snake Alley Art Show, artists' booths line the street that scales the river bluff in Burlington, Iowa.

furnishings; and the Apple Trees Museum at 1616 Dill St., with local history displays (319/753-2449). Arts for Living Center—Built just after the Civil War, this church at Seventh St. and Washington St. houses an art gallery and gift shop featuring original works by local artists (319/754-8069).

RECREATION

Crapo Park—Visit the bluff where explorer Zebulon Pike first raised the American flag on Iowa soil in 1805. Grandpa Bill's Farm— A century-old farmstead is now a 100-acre park with water slides, a swimming beach, fishing and boating, and camping and picnicking facilities. The farm is located about 12 miles north of Burlington on US-61 (319/985-2262).

FESTIVALS

Burlington Steamboat Days—Top rock, country, jazz, big band and blues acts perform on outdoor stages in mid-June. That same weekend, the picturesque Snake Alley neighborhood hosts a popular regional arts fair (800/827-4837).

Keokuk, Iowa

The hillside city of Keokuk anchors Iowa's southeast corner. Its site at the confluence of the Mississippi and Des Moines rivers made the area a natural center for commerce, despite dangerous rapids.

During the Civil War, Keokuk played a vital role as the central swearing-in point for Iowa volunteers and as a major medical center for those wounded on southern battlefields. Many soldiers who didn't survive are buried in Keokuk's National Cemetery, one of the original 12 established by Congress. Keokuk also takes pride in its Mark Twain connection: Samuel Clemens worked in his brother's printing shop here after leaving Hannibal. Today, this city of 13,000 is known for many homes overlooking the Mississippi.

To get to Keokuk from Nauvoo, take IL State-96 south for 11 miles, then cross the Mississippi River at Hamilton. For more information, contact: Keokuk Convention & Visitors Bureau (800/383-1219).

LODGINGS

Grand Anne Bed & Breakfast—This impressive Queen Anne-style mansion, built in 1897, sits on a high bluff above the Mississippi. For breakfast, feast on homemade cinnamon rolls. Doubles from $65 (319/524-6310 or 800/524-6310). The River's Edge—There's a European flavor to the decor of this 1915 Tudor-style home. Doubles from $75 (319/524-1700).

DINING

Liz Clark's—People eagerly attend this nationally-known cooking school and reservation-only gourmet restaurant. One of the area's leading magnates built the mansion (319/524-4716).

SIGHTSEEING

Keokuk's 1,900-foot lock and dam are among the biggest on the river. Tours of the adjoining hydroelectric plant are offered from Memorial Day through Labor Day (319/524-9660). George M. Verity Riverboat Museum—The 1927 stern-wheeler along the riverfront in Victory Park displays exhibits about Mississippi River history (319/524-4765). Samuel F. Miller House and Museum— A Supreme Court justice appointed by President Lincoln once owned this home at 318 N. Fifth St. (319/524-5599). Rand Park—Stop by the burial site of well-known Chief Keokuk of the Sac and Fox tribes for whom the city is named. The site overlooks the Mississippi at 17th St. and Grand Ave.

FESTIVALS

Bald Eagle Appreciation Days—Each January, Keokuk celebrates the birds that winter here. The Battle of Pea Ridge Civil War Reenactment— Held in April, it's one of the Midwest's largest events of this type.

By Lori Erickson

QUINCY

Tree-lined streets and grand old houses recall hometowns across the Heartland.

Quincy boasts street after street of lovely old homes.

Mark Twain describes Quincy, Illinois, in words that seem as true today as when he penned them in the 1880s: Quincy, Twain proclaimed, is a "brisk, handsome, well-ordered city … interested in art, letters, and other high things."

Perched on a bluff above the Mississippi River's largest natural harbor, prosperous early Quincy earned the nickname "Gem City" for its splendid homes and commercial success. Today, with its architectural excellence and cultural pursuits intact, this Heartland town welcomes visitors to share its interpretation of the good life.

Artful Living

Nearly 40 arts organizations, from the Muddy River Opera Company to the Quincy China Painters, thrive in this community of 45,000, where per capita support of the arts is the highest of any city in the country. Visitors quickly discover that the arts are a way of life in Quincy. The bed-and-breakfast owner sings tenor in the Great River Barbershop Chorus, the police lieutenant is the principal tuba in the Quincy Symphony Orchestra, and everybody is a booster.

Such community involvement helped the city win the prestigious Illinois Governor's Award for Volunteerism, an honor that recognizes Quincy citizens' extraordinary commitment to the quality of life in their riverside city.

Visitors quickly get information about the local arts scene by picking up a copy of the free glossy monthly magazine *Arts/Quincy*. It details entertainment ranging from the Early Music Consort and the Mississippi River Brass Band to the Jazz Cabaret at Quincy University.

The Gem City's Architecture

Artistic flair also embellishes historical buildings that line Quincy's streets. The city boasts the state's finest collection of architectural treasures outside of Chicago. The National Register of Historic Places lists more than 2,000 buildings in Quincy's three historic districts. Booklets for pleasant self-guided walking tours will lead you through the city's most significant areas.

One district, dominated by Quincy's southside

RUSS MUNN

German neighborhoods, is a charming collection of modest brick homes. Another district is distinguished by majestic homes in the tree-lined East End, an area that includes an intersection at Maine and 16th streets that *National Geographic* magazine once dubbed "the most architecturally significant corner in America."

The third district centers around Washington Park downtown, the city's original central square. Twelve thousand people turned out to hear Abraham Lincoln and Stephen Douglas debate in the leafy square in 1858. The town memorialized the event with a bronze bas-relief plaque by famed Illinois-born sculptor Lorado Taft.

After you've seen Quincy's historic neighborhoods, visit the Gardner Museum of Architecture and Design. At this Romanesque-style structure that stands like a small castle near Washington Park, you can examine the bits and pieces of the city's lost architectural treasures. Outside, run your hand over deeply carved cornerstones and cornices displayed in the small garden. Inside, climb the stairs to the second story to marvel at jewel-tone stained-glass windows from long-ago churches. Black-and-white photos document the destruction in the 1960s of a monumental train station, an event that rallied the town to preserve its remaining architectural heritage.

From the Gardner Museum, drive east on Maine Street to another

The home of Quincy's founder, Governor John Wood, is now a museum.

JUDITH P. KNUTH

A regal 1890s mansion houses The Quincy Museum.

JUDITH P. KNUTH

Romanesque beauty, the buff-colored stone mansion that houses the Quincy Museum. When the palatial home was built in 1891, a local newspaper noted, "For elegance of architectural design and beauty of construction, it is a home which cannot be surpassed in any city, east or west." The restored first floor looks unchanged since its original owners, the Newcombs, lived there. The massive fireplaces, mahogany paneling and stained-glass windows are warm and inviting, despite their grandeur. On the upper floors, displays of local history, geology and natural history draw visiting schoolchildren.

Across the street on the grounds of another mansion, the Quincy Arts Center has found a home in the expanded carriage house. Exhibits spotlight works by artists from the immediate area, as well as contemporary pieces by artists across the Midwest. A few blocks south on 12th Street is another architectural landmark, the Governor John Wood Mansion. Wood, who was both Quincy's founder and the 12th governor of Illinois, lived in this imposing Greek Revival home.

Of all the architecture in Quincy, perhaps none is so remarkable as the extraordinary house that perches atop a bluff overlooking the river just south of

downtown. From a distance, the Moorish-style structure, called Villa Kathrine, looks like a mirage from an Arabian Nights fantasy. George Metz, a wealthy bon vivant with an exotic taste for Arabic architecture, built it in 1900. The restored mansion now houses a tourist information center. The interior is unfurnished but strikingly detailed, with a tiled reflecting pool and exotic woodwork. Visitors may tour the rooms that once housed Metz and his sole companion, a 200-pound mastiff dog named Bingo.

Day's End On the River

Let your day wind down in Quincy with a view of the sun setting across the Mississippi. You may want to head to bluff-top Riverview Park to share the vista with the handsome statue of explorer George Rogers Clark. Or watch the sun go down while savoring catfish fillet at The Pier Restaurant, where the glass-walled dining room faces the Mississippi. Finally, consider a picnic supper in the gazebo at Clat Adams Bicentennial Park. Set on the riverbank near the base of two bridges leading to Missouri, the park's plantings and cobblestone walks make it a favorite spot for locals and tourists.

Planning Your Visit to Quincy

For more information, contact: Quincy Convention & Visitors Bureau (217/223-1000); Tourist Information Center (217/224-3688).

LODGINGS

Choose from among Quincy's dozen motels, including well-known chains and mom-and-pop operations, with doubles ranging from $25 to $80. Bed and breakfasts listed are all in the historic district:

The Kaufmann House—Quincy's history is on display at the town's oldest bed and breakfast, with framed artwork relating to owners Bettie and Emery Kaufmann's longtime family connections to the area. Choose from a trio of charming guest rooms and relax in the shady, secluded garden. Doubles from $50 (217/223-2502).

The Dashwood House—Dogwoods and a magnificent magnolia tree surround this 1907 white clapboard Greek Revival-style home. Breakfast includes fresh scones and delicious homemade lemon curd. Well-behaved canines Fibber McGee and Molly greet guests. Doubles from $45 (217/223-1430).

The Bueltmann Gasthaus—From the imported lace curtains in the Edelweiss room to the German apple pancakes served at breakfast, a German theme prevails. The original 1880s Queen Anne-style home was updated with English Tudor styling in the 1920s. The result is a homey hybrid in creamy stone and chocolate stucco. Doubles from $65 (217/224-8428).

DINING

The Pier Restaurant—Arching over the edge of the riverbank, this octagon-shaped contemporary restaurant with a bright blue roof gives diners close-up views of passing river traffic. Inside, patrons

A lush garden surrounds The Kaufmann House, a bed and breakfast in Quincy's Main Street historic district.

JUDITH P. KNUTH

admire historic photos of Quincy and a model of a steam engine paddle-boat. The menu features catfish, with prime rib a weekend favorite (217/221-0020).

Tiramisu—This sophisticated Italian eatery downtown is named for the luscious Italian dessert that combines creamy cheese with rum-soaked sponge cake. Owner Roberto Stellino recommends the fettucini with salmon sauce, rigatoni with fresh spinach, and, of course, "the best tiramisu you can get" (217/222-9560).

The Lakeview Restaurant—Set on a small lake on the east side of town, this casual restaurant has an aquarium in the dining room. It's known for seafood, particularly yellow fin tuna and salmon made to order: broiled, fried or grilled. There's alfresco dining on the patio when the weather permits (217/222-9661).

The Ritz—Locals like this traditional downtown spot across from the Holiday Inn for its dark wood interiors and fireplace, as well as the steaks and barbecue ribs (217/222-8122).

C.J.'s Coffee—Expect a good breakfast or lunch.

At midday, try breads and desserts baked on the premises, as well as homemade soups, such as tomato Florentine and cheese-broccoli (217/223-3333).

SIGHTSEEING

All Wars Museum—Set on the wooded grounds of the Illinois Veterans Home, one of the oldest such institutions in the country, the museum's exhibits recall military conflicts from the American Revolution to the Gulf War. Among the displays are military uniforms, medals and models of World War II battleships and aircraft (217/222-8641).

Dr. Richard Eell's House—Originally owned by an early Quincy physician, this two-story red brick home dating to the 1830s was considered the number one stop on the Underground Railroad for slaves escaping from Missouri towns. Book tours by appointment only (217/222-1799).

Gardner Museum of Architecture and Design—The handsome turn-of-the-century Romanesque building, formerly a public library, offers wide-ranging temporary exhibits, along with permanent displays on stained glass and design and an outdoor area with artifacts. Check the gift shop for unusual decorative objects crafted from architectural remnants (217/224-6873).

Governor John Wood Mansion—One of the finest examples of Greek Revival architecture in the Midwest, this imposing 14-room home was built in the 1830s by the

JUDITH P. KNUTH

Self-guided driving or walking tours lead visitors past Quincy's historic residences.

German craftsmen and stonemasons who helped to settle Quincy. The mansion was the home of Quincy's founder, John Wood, who became Illinois governor in 1860. Originally built about a block west of its current location, the house was moved to its present site in the 1860s, no small feat for a structure of this size. It's furnished with Wood family heirlooms and local memorabilia (217/222-1835).

Quincy Art Center—The small art center has studio space, an ambitious schedule of workshops and classes, and changing exhibitions featuring local, Midwest and nationally-known artists. The center's premises are extraordinary: an expanded carriage house topped by a cupola and weather vane. Joseph Silsbee designed the original portion of the picturesque 19th-century structure. Interestingly, Frank Lloyd Wright received his first architectural training in Silsbee's office (217/223-5900).

Quincy Museum—A sprawling stone mansion with a broad, welcoming porch and massive red-roofed turrets houses a diverse collection. Interior architectural details on the first floor include wood paneling and a hand-painted frieze in the dining room. Upper floors focus on various historical eras dating to the dinosaurs (217/224-7669).

Lincoln-Douglas Valentine Museum—Many of the sweets-to-the-sweet boxes of chocolates given on Valentine's Day through the years were made at the Quincy Paper Box factory. Heart-shaped and covered in red satin, these sentimental symbols are on display, along with elaborate paper valentines. The small downtown museum is open daily by appointment (217/224-3355 or 217/224-8763).

TRAVEL GUIDE

Villa Kathrine—Romantic stories persist about the odd and lovely building that now serves as Quincy's Tourist Information Center. Native Quincyan and intrepid traveler George Metz built the bluff-top villa in 1900, basing its design on photographs and sketches he made on his journeys through Arabic lands. Some say he meant it as a memorial to his mother, Catherine; others believe it became a sad monument to a lost love, Katherine, who died before the building was completed (217/224-3688).

SHOPPING

Osage Orangerie Gift Shop—Located in the visitors center of the Governor John Wood Mansion and named for the onetime governor who maintained rows of orange trees, the gift shop features the work of local craftspeople and sells antiques on consignment (217/222-1835). The Briar Patch—A modern, rustic-style log cabin with a 10,000-gallon freshwater aquarium is the setting for a craft mall featuring 60 booths. Dealers showcase such items as wood shelves, handmade clothing and dolls (217/223-6130). Quincy Steamboat Company—Tucked into a quiet street just southwest of downtown is a

combination cooking school/gourmet shop brimming with specialty cookware, hard-to-find spices, jars of luscious sauces and jams, and other gifts for the family chef (217/224-6644). Yester Year Antique Mall— In a vintage brick J. C. Penney building downtown, this 15,000-square foot mall houses 50 dealers selling all sorts of items, such as furniture, silver, vintage advertising memorabilia and books about collectibles. Pick up brochures that list other antiques shops in Quincy (217/224-1871).

OUTDOOR RECREATION

Clat Adams Park—Head down to the river at Front St. and Hampshire

JUDITH P. KNUTH

Visit Riverview Park to share George Rogers Clark's bluff-top view of the Mississippi River.

St. to access this neat-as-a-pin park with close-up views of the old and new bridges, one carrying traffic west to the Missouri side, the other going east.

Gardner Division of the Mark Twain National Wildlife Refuge— Dedicated to preserving wetlands along the river, the refuge sprawls over 6,000 acres just north of Quincy. Side channels serve as habitats for deer and turkey. Large numbers of waterfowl fill the sky during migrations; songbirds and warblers attract bird-watchers in the spring. Bear Creek Campground is located at the north end (573/847-2333 or 217/224-8580).

FESTIVALS & ANNUAL EVENTS

For information on all annual events and festivals, contact: Quincy Convention & Visitors Bureau (217/223-1000). Dogwood Festival— Downtown's Washington Park is the scene of a festival during the first weekend in May. Residents welcome spring with a parade, food vendors, live music and a craft fair. World Free Fall Convention—Skies over Quincy bloom with startling color and motion at the annual early August skydiving convention that attracts 4,500 skydivers to the Quincy Municipal Airport. Visitors can participate in tandem dives and take helicopter and hot-air balloon rides. The event honors the memory of Quincy's native son,

Thomas Baldwin, who first parachuted from a hot-air balloon here in 1887, then went on to design the U.S. government's first dirigible.

Germanfest—Quincy celebrates its German heritage the last weekend in June with oompah bands, lively dancing, hearty Old World dishes and children's rides in South Park.

Early Tin Dusters Annual Color Run—More than 600 vintage cars show up and show off at this October event featuring antique and vintage autos. The colorful gathering and charity event, held in Uptown Quincy and Upper Moorman Park, has been a tradition since 1975 (217/964-2426).

Quincy Preserves—Historic homes open their doors for tours during this event in mid- to late October. Later in the year, some of the town's finest old homes open for candlelight tours during the holiday season in mid-December.

OTHER PLACES TO VISIT
IN THE AREA
For more information on the area, contact: Western Illinois Tourism Development Office (309/837-7460).

SIGHTSEEING &
ENTERTAINMENT
Fort Edwards State Memorial—Two early forts stood guard over the river in Warsaw, 30 miles north of Quincy in Illinois. A concrete pillar marks the site of the forts, the second of which became a center for trade with Sac and Fox Indians.

Perched on a bluff overlooking the river, the exotic Villa Kathrine is now a visitors center.

Prairie Mills Windmill Golden Historical and Museum—This mock windmill, 20 miles northeast of Quincy, dates to 1872. The original grinding stones and wooden gears are still in place. The museum's displays document pioneer life on the Illinois prairie (217/696-4672).

St. Patrick, Missouri—The post office in this tiny town (population 17) cancels thousands of greeting cards each March. Visit the Shrine of St. Patrick, a church splendidly decorated with ancient Celtic motifs. The Old Irish Antique and Gift Shop stocks Irish imports (816/754-6198).

Old Carthage Jail & Visitors Center—Where colorful Mormon leader Joseph Smith went, trouble followed. This site in Carthage, 45 miles northeast of Quincy, marks the spot where Smith and his brother, Hyrum, were killed by a mob in 1844. The Mormons fled from nearby Nauvoo to Salt Lake City, Utah (217/357-2989).

Kibbe Museum—In a newly built modern structure next to City Hall, the Kibbe Museum in Carthage, Illinois, displays Civil War and Indian artifacts, period fashion and toys, and natural history items. (217/357-3119).

OUTDOOR RECREATION
Siloam Springs State Park—Victorians patronized the park, believing its spring water had health-giving properties. Today, it's one of the largest parks in Illinois, with a lake, 12 miles of hiking trails, camping, boating, fishing and picnic areas (217/894-6205).

Wakonda State Park—Six small lakes offer boat rentals and swimming in this scenic wooded acreage across the river from Quincy (573/655-2280).

By Lori Erickson and Judith P. Knuth

HANNIBAL

Have a rollicking good time in Tom Sawyer and Huck Finn's hometown.

Samuel Langhorne Clemens left Hannibal, Missouri, years before he gained fame as the acclaimed author Mark Twain, but he never forgot the small Mississippi River village in northeast Missouri where he grew up. Twain gave his boyhood friends and haunts new life as characters and places in *The Adventures of Tom Sawyer* and *The Adventures of Huckleberry Finn*. For visitors today, strolling Hannibal's streets and soaking up its local color is like slipping between the covers of those beloved books.

A Spirited Port City

Founded in 1819, Hannibal was a lively river port by the time the Clemens family moved here from nearby Florida, Missouri, in 1839. Young Sam was four years old. During his youth in the 1840s and 1850s, steamboats paraded up and down the Mississippi River. In 1849 alone, 1,200 gaily-painted paddle- and side-wheelers docked in Hannibal, each signaling its arrival with shrill blasts from a steam whistle. Every day, farmers, merchants and townsfolk crowded the docks, greeting arriving passengers and watching eagerly for newspapers, mail and merchandise arriving from big cities.

In Twain's day, the rough and rowdy commercial district along the Mississippi bristled with a seedy army of river tramps. They fascinated the young Sam Clemens with tales of their exploits, and he later returned the favor by making a pair of unsavory river characters, the King and the Duke, central players in *Huckleberry Finn*.

Many of Twain's Hannibal memories found their way into his works, so it's not surprising that the town seems familiar to the 600,000 visitors who flock here each year. The modest two-story white clapboard house where Twain grew up became Aunt Polly's house in his stories. His father's law office across the street inspired the fictional setting of Muff Potter's trial. Young Sam Clemens' personal landmarks became the territory of his characters. Tom Sawyer and Huck Finn wandered Cardiff Hill and Inspiration Point in the course of many adventures. Injun Joe hid and later died in the mazelike cave south of Hannibal.

CHET HANCHETT

Whitewashing contestants make their brushes fly.

The Past Preserved

The town now numbers 18,000 citizens instead of 4,000 as it did in Twain's day. But its tidy streets and expansive river views strike countless chords with anyone who loves the author's books.

The Mark Twain Boyhood Home and Museum forms the centerpiece of a downtown historical area that covers 11 blocks (four of which contain most of the Twain-related sites). More than 8 million people have visited the house since Twain's death in 1910. Each year visitors from nearly 100 nations sign the home's guest book. For more proof of his books' continuing popularity, simply step outside the house to see the crowds clustered around its famous whitewashed fence, the town's favorite picture-taking spot.

Next door is one of the town's two Mark Twain museums. See the memorabilia here, then head down the street two blocks to the new museum, where you can view 16 charming paintings by Norman Rockwell that once illustrated editions of Twain's timeless stories.

Just down the street, the lure of the river makes a ride on the *Mark Twain* excursion boat a must for visitors. From May through October, this replica of an old-time riverboat cruises on daily sightseeing loops from the Wabash Railroad Bridge south to Inspiration Point. The boat offers front-seat views of Hannibal's waterfront, with its cobbled landing, marina, exercise path and tidy park. Visitors can relax on benches and gaze at the river. Once ashore, take a horse-drawn carriage ride along Main Street, which parallels the river through the historic district.

Twain's Books Live On

Shops housed in restored 19th-century buildings along Main Street attract visitors. The names of Twain and his characters seem to pop up everywhere.

Visitors may sleep at the Hotel Clemens, lunch at Huck's Homestead, shop at Mrs. Clemens Antique Mall and thumb through volumes by and about Twain at Becky Thatcher's Bookstore. (The store was once the home of Sam Clemens' schoolmate, Laura Hawkins, the inspiration for young Becky.)

A mile south of Hannibal lies the Mark Twain Cave, once a playground for the adventurous young Sam. Twain's Tom and Becky were lost in damp, narrow passages that twisted and turned for miles. They clutched hands and comforted each other, while Tom

Tom and Huck at the Mark Twain Outdoor Theater.

FRANK OBERLE

19th-century buildings along Hannibal's Main Street.

feared his enemy, Injun Joe, crouched somewhere nearby in the inky darkness. Today, tour groups deep within the cool limestone cavern gasp as their guides douse the lights.

More Twain sites are within an easy drive or walk. A statue of Twain gazes out on the river from the 300-foot bluff at Riverview Park, a fine picnic spot north of downtown. A frequently photographed statue of Tom and Huck stands at the base of a flight of steps that scales Cardiff Hill. High above the statue is The Mark Twain Lighthouse, erected in 1935 on the centennial of his birth.

When evening comes, visitors head to an amphitheater south of town to watch *The Reflections of Mark Twain* outdoor pageant, a drama about the author and his characters. The Molly Brown Dinner Theatre features an evening of song and dance. The establishment is dedicated to the memory of Hannibal's second-most-famous citizen. Born in 1867, Molly Brown amassed wealth in Colorado, gained fame as an art connoisseur and world traveler, and worked tirelessly for charities. The Broadway musical and film, *The Unsinkable Molly Brown*, celebrated her life.

At its busiest, Hannibal has a carnival air, bustling with people and contradicting Twain's description of his boyhood home as "a white town drowsing in the sun." The town's exuberance peaks during National Tom Sawyer Days each July Fourth weekend. More than 100,000 people join in frog-jumping and fence-whitewashing contests, listen to country bands and inspect arts-and-crafts booths. There are even watermelon-seed spitting competitions. The fun includes the crowning of the town's official Tom and Becky, seventh graders who serve as goodwill ambassadors for the year. (Tom's scepter is a cane fishing pole, and Becky's is a slate chalkboard.) Busy hands grasping brushes create a mist of whitewash, while boys and girls coax and prod bullfrogs to jump. No one can resist the fun inspired by Mark Twain's fiction.

The festivities probably would amuse the author. Remarking on his popularity, Twain once said, "My books are water, those of great geniuses are wine. Everybody drinks water."

If you're a Mark Twain fan, a visit to Hannibal will help quench your thirst, whether you prefer water or wine.

TRAVEL GUIDE

Planning Your Visit to Hannibal

For help in planning your visit, contact: The Hannibal Convention & Visitors Bureau (573/221-2477). For general travel information, contact: Missouri Div. of Tourism (800/877-1234 or 573/751-4133).

LODGING

Hannibal's 10 motels include national chains, with doubles ranging from $40 to $100. Bed and breakfasts include:

Fifth Street Mansion— Step back in time by booking a room in this 1858 Italianate home (213 S. Fifth St.) with antique furnishings, stained-glass windows and original fireplaces. Seven guest rooms are available, including full breakfast. Doubles from $70 (800/874-5661 or 573/221-0445).

Garth Woodside Mansion—Rated one of the 10 best inns in the Midwest, this 1871 country estate sits on 39 wooded acres. French toast with fresh peach sauce is a specialty of the house. Doubles from $77 (573/221-2789).

Queen Anne's Grace— Overlooking the town from a hillside is an 1880s Victorian mansion at 313 N. Fifth St. There are two suites,

as well as one guest room. Doubles from $77 (573/248-0756).

Cliffside Mansion— Adjacent to historic Rockcliffe Mansion, this English-style home (#8 Stillwell Pl.) offers seven guest rooms, some with shared baths. Doubles from $55 (573/248-1461).

DINING

Hearty home-style cooking tops the menus at many Hannibal restaurants.

Huck's Homestead Restaurant— Four miles south of Hannibal on US-61, you can eat heartily from a nightly buffet of fried chicken, catfish and all the trimmings (573/985-5961).

Fourth of July frog-jumping contests in Hannibal recall one of Mark Twain's earliest stories.

Riverview Cafe at Sawyer's Creek— On State-79 S., this restaurant overlooks the Mississippi River and specializes in

family-style fare (573/221-8292).

Ole Planters Restaurant— Located on North Main in the historic district, this eatery is best known for its pork tenderloins and pies (573/221-4410).

Mark Twain Riverboat— Dine on sirloin of beef and baked chicken during evening dinner cruises. Board the boat in the historic district at the foot of Center St. (573/221-3222).

SIGHTSEEING

Mark Twain made Hannibal famous, but timber and concrete brought the town wealth in its early years. The homes of early industrialists line hillside streets overlooking the river. At the Hannibal Convention & Visitors Bureau at 505 N. Third St., you can pick up a historic-homes brochure that makes a good guide for either a car or walking tour. Hannibal's most palatial home, the 30-room Rockcliffe Mansion at 1000 Bird St., is open daily to visitors (573/221-4140). Major Twain-related sites include the Mark Twain Boyhood Home and Museum (573/221-9010) at 208 Hill St. and the Mark Twain Cave (573/221-1656) on State-79, 1 mile south of Hannibal. Both are open year-round. The

The early history of the region is preserved In the Culler cabin in the utopian German community of Bethel.

Mark Twain Riverboat docks at the foot of Center St. and cruises May through October (573/221-3222). Tours of the area are available on the *Twainland Express* (800/786-5193 or 573/221-5593) or *Hannibal Trolley* (573/221-1161), both of which depart from the downtown area.
The Optical Science Center and Museum at 214 N. Main St. (573/ 221-2020) provides hands-on exhibits and a computerized light show.

THEATER
The Molly Brown Dinner Theatre, at 200 N. Main St., stages luncheon and dinner shows (573/221-8940). The Mark Twain Outdoor Theatre, on US-61 S., stages nightly performances June through August (573/221-2945 or 573/985-3581).

FAMILY FUN
Sawyer's Creek Fun Park, an amusement center with children's rides, miniature golf and gift shops, lies overlooking the Mississippi River across from Mark Twain Cave on State-79 S. (573/221-8221).

SHOPPING
Native American Trading Company & Gallery at 208 North St. sells hand-crafted items from a variety of native tribes (573/248-3451). Mississippi Dry Goods at 217 N. Main St. offers 4,000 square feet of antiques, primitives, crafts and gifts (573/221-1799).

FESTIVALS
National Tom Sawyer Days—An extravaganza of fence-whitewashing, frog-jumping and other contests happens over the July Fourth weekend. Autumn Historic Folklife Festival, when artisans demonstrate lifestyles and crafts of the 19th century, is in mid-October. Beginning in late November, Christmas in Hannibal includes carolers strolling decorated streets, holiday lighting and weekend events (573/221-2477).

OTHER PLACES TO VISIT IN THE AREA
Mark Twain Lake
The two-room cabin where Samuel Clemens was born in 1835 is preserved within Mark Twain State Park, which lies 20 miles southwest of Hannibal. The park overlooks Mark Twain Lake, Missouri's newest major reservoir. The 18,600-acre lake is lined with marinas, boat ramps and swimming beaches and is known for outstanding crappie and bass fishing. The surrounding rolling hills and rock bluffs contain 450 campsites. For information, contact: Mark Twain Lake Chamber of Commerce, P.O. Box 59, Perry, MO 63462 (573/565-2228).
The small town of Monroe City, located just north of the lake, is home to The Landing Recreational Resort, which includes a water park, camping areas, restaurant and amusement park (573/735-4242).

Bethel, Missouri
Sam Clemens was 9 years old in 1844, the year German immigrant Wilhelm Keil founded

The colorful riverboat Mark Twain *makes daily sightseeing cruises along Hannibal's riverfront.*

Bethel, his utopian colony 48 miles northwest of Hannibal. The charismatic leader and many members of the Christian commune left Missouri for Oregon in 1855, but about 100 descendants of the original colonists still call Bethel home.

During the summer, The School of the Arts conducts one-week classes teaching crafts, such as weaving and natural dyeing, and lessons in fiddling and playing the hammered dulcimer and parlor piano.

Try to schedule your visit during one of Bethel's many weekend festivals (from Hannibal, take US-36 west to State-15, then turn north). In June, fiddlers from across the Heartland play at the Fiddle Fest. There's a Sheep Fest featuring shearing, weaving and spinning on Labor Day; a Harvest Fest in October; and Christmas in Bethel celebration in early December.

Bethel also opens its 19th-century doors for home tours. Downtown you can watch clay being shaped at SJ Pottery and shop for crafts at the Gift Shop, which doubles as the local museum. Make sure to stop at Bethel's renowned Fest Hall Restaurant (816/284-6493). Home-style cooking, such as smothered steak, salmon patties, fruit pies, and cream pies, draws visitors. On festival days, the menu includes Old World standards such as bratwurst and sauerkraut. Upstairs are four simply furnished guest rooms. Doubles from $30, including a full breakfast.

For information, contact: Historic Bethel German Colony, Box 127, Bethel, MO 63434 (816/284-6493).

Palmyra, Missouri

Palmyra, a town of 3,400 located 10 miles northwest of Hannibal, was billed as the "handsomest city in north Missouri" in Civil War days. The town boasts a wealth of pre-Civil War architecture, including the 1828 Gardener House. Once a stagecoach stop and hotel, it now serves as an information center and local history museum (573/769-3076). Outside the tan brick courthouse stands a monument to 10 Confederate solders executed there in 1862. William Russell, founder of the Pony Express, lies buried in the cemetery north of town. For more information, contact: Palmyra Chamber of Commerce, 301 S. Main St., Palmyra, MO 63461 (573/769-2223).

Louisiana, Missouri

In Louisiana, Missouri, 25 miles south of Hannibal, the star attraction is the Stark Bro's Nurseries. Founded in 1816, the nationally-prominent

Mark Twain's Boyhood Home and Museum *attract readers of his work from around the world.*

nursery lies on the western edge of town. Across the street sits the cabin that founder James Stark built in 1816. Visit in early August and you can feast on juicy Missouri peaches.

This small town of 4,000 is also home to many gracious antebellum homes built by the southerners from Kentucky, Virginia, Tennessee and the Carolinas who founded the town in 1818. The downtown has a Victorian air, and Henderson-Riverview Park offers scenic views of the Mississippi. The Louisiana Historical Museum at 304 Georgia St. is a good spot to stop for information on local history (573/754-5550).

LODGINGS

Riverview Bed and Breakfast—Built in the 1880s atop a bluff overlooking the Mississippi River, this four guest-room bed and breakfast has shared baths. Fragrant homemade cinnamon rolls top its breakfast menu. Doubles from $60 (573/754-4270).

Serandos House—This Victorian home, built in the 1870s at 918 Georgia St., offers two guest rooms. A full breakfast includes freshly baked breads. Doubles from $65 (800/754-4067).

For more information,

contact: Louisiana Chamber of Commerce (573/754-5921).

Clarksville, Missouri

Thirty-five miles south of Hannibal lies Clarksville, a charming town of 500

settled in 1817. Many of its buildings are listed in the National Register of Historic Places, and the town is known for its craft and antiques stores. The Clarksville Eagle Center (573/242-3132) is a satellite of the St. Louis-based World Bird Sanctuary. You'll see live eagles here, as well as exhibits on other birds and animals. The workings of Lock and Dam No. 24, part of the system that keeps the Mississippi navigable for barge traffic, are visible through the Eagle Center's windows.

The open waters of the dam make this prime feeding ground for bald eagles in winter. Each year on the last two

weekends in January, Clarksville's Eagle Days feature bird-viewing and conservation programs. On the third weekend in September, it's Big River Days. Visitors can hitch a ride on a U.S. Corps of Engineers towboat, mingle

FRANK OBERLE

A chairlift takes visitors to the top of Lookout Point in Clarksville, the river's highest bluff south of St. Paul.

with Civil War reenactors and celebrate the end of a hot Missouri summer with good food and drink.

LODGINGS

Rosemont Farm Bed & Breakfast—This 160-acre 1854 farm nestled in rolling hills 8 miles south of Clarksville has the gracious air of an old southern home. Of three guest rooms, one has a private bath. Expect a breakfast of fresh fruit and Belgian waffles served on Royal Doulton china. Doubles from $65 (573/847-2219).

For more information, contact: Clarksville Chamber of Commerce (573/242-3993).

By Lori Erickson

ALTON, ELSAH AND GRAFTON

Three welcoming river towns on Illinois' western border share a spectacular setting.

Two-thirds of the way down Illinois' western border, the southbound Mississippi River curls languidly to the east and meets the Illinois River. The confluence energizes the Mississippi. Its powerful flow has carved limestone bluffs that tower like massive sentinels above the broad channel. The dramatic vista awed early explorers in the area and still draws modern-day travelers to the old river towns of Alton, Elsah and Grafton.

A Proud Past Remembered

St. Louis and Alton face each other across the Mississippi, twin links in America's relentless journey west. In the 1830s, ferryboats crowded with westward-bound pioneers churned across the river at Alton. Soon, the little town's prosperity rivaled that of its much larger across-the-river neighbor. Handsome Federal-style brick homes sprang up along the streets that climbed Alton's river bluffs, and riverfront merchants thrived.

The steamboats that once docked at Alton have long since departed. Today, downtown bustles with other kinds of activities. Over 60 antiques shops, restaurants, sidewalk cafes and art galleries line the steep hills above the riverfront, making this a mecca for shoppers. At the riverfront itself glitters Alton Belle Casino, docked just above the new Clark Bridge that gracefully spans the river into St. Louis.

History buffs can trace the personalities and events of Alton's past in the town's museums and public sculpture. The statue of Elijah P. Lovejoy at Fifth and Monument streets recalls a dramatic and turbulent time in the nation's history. In opposition to thriving mid-19th-century slave markets in St. Louis, antislavery factions made Alton a major stop on the Underground Railroad. In 1837, a proslavery mob killed Lovejoy, an abolitionist newspaper editor.

A pair of statues at Broadway and Market streets marks a clash that occurred two decades later. Abraham Lincoln and Stephen Douglas, candidates to represent Illinois in the Senate, squared off in their final debate. Lincoln "thrashed out" Douglas, reported the local paper. The loser, however, eventually won the Illinois senate race. Sculptures of the great debaters

THOMAS D. WATKINS PHOTOGRAPHY

Redbuds frame Elsah's village hall.

stand in Lincoln-Douglas Square. Across town, the Alton Museum of History and Art offers more information about the city's past.

Enchanting Elsah

Travelers heading north from Alton can follow either the Great River Road (State-100) or the adjoining bike path, both of which hug the narrow strip of land between the river and cliffs. Ten miles upriver lies the tiny village of Elsah, the first town listed in its entirety in the National Register of Historic Places. Once a busy river port, Elsah slumbered through much of the 20th century after the steamboat industry died. Its immaculately kept stone cottages and narrow streets exude a New England air, with glorious gardens blooming behind picket fences.

Wander the streets of Elsah, where history quietly lingers. Victorian-style hats and jewelry are specialties at the Somewhere in Time Gift Shop on the main floor of the Green Tree Inn, a bed and breakfast along Mill Street. Just up the hill along upper LaSalle Street, the Maple Leaf Cottage Inn provides a peaceful overnight getaway amid beautiful gardens.

Take time to stroll the picturesque campus of Principia, the world's only Christian Science college. Covering 2,500 acres, the campus sits on a bluff overlooking the Mississippi. The college's bluff-colored cottages, Tudor half-timber buildings and lovely chapel bring to mind an English village.

On to Grafton

A 19th-century ambience prevails in Grafton, 5 miles north of Elsah on the Great River Road. Its strategic location at the confluence of the Illinois and Mississippi rivers lured early settlers, though the waterways periodically brought flooding, as well as commerce.

The statue of Robert Wadlow, the tallest man who ever lived.

ROBERT PERSHING WADLOW
FEBRUARY 22, 1918 — JULY 15, 1940

Fish is on the menu and in the aquariums at the Fin Inn in Grafton.

Most recently, the great flood of 1993 damaged many homes and businesses in Grafton, but the town's indomitable spirit prevailed.

Grafton's newly restored Ruebel Hotel takes center stage in the downtown historic district. Established in 1884 and once a busy watering hole for steamboat pilots and passengers, the 23-room Ruebel shines again with Victorian splendor. Burgundy carpets, brocade wall coverings and elegant wood stairways make a rich design statement. Guests can relax in a hot tub overlooking the river. In the Ruebel Saloon, dining patrons gather around a burled walnut bar purchased at the St. Louis World's Fair in 1904.

Curio shops, antiques stores and bed and breakfasts sit along State-100, the town's main street. Drop by the Fin Inn, where guests seem to dine nose-to-nose with fish and turtles swimming in three 2,000-gallon aquariums. At the Country Corner Fudge Shop, they'll entice you with a sample of their rich chocolate treats, then rent you a bike so you can pedal off the calories. On the bluff above Grafton perches the Tara Point

Inn, an intimate, contemporary-style retreat. From this vantage point on a clear day, you can glimpse the St. Louis Gateway Arch 30 miles away.

Lush woods laced with 15 miles of hiking trails await visitors to the 8,000-acre Père Marquette State Park, 5 miles to the north of Grafton on Highway 100. The park's name honors Father Jacques Marquette, who in 1673, along with Louis Joliet, reached the Illinois River where it meets the Mississippi. A 700-ton stone fireplace in the lobby blazes a warm welcome to the park's stone-and-log lodge, where guests overnight in rooms overlooking the Illinois River or the surrounding woods.

For a taste of nature's abundance throughout summer and fall, stop by area roadside stands overflowing with fruits from the orchards in surrounding Jersey and Calhoun counties. Succulent peaches, crisp apples and a cornucopia of berries testify to the richness of the soil laid down by the Mississippi River over thousands of years. The bountiful harvest provides one more reason to visit and savor this section of the Great River Road.

TRAVEL GUIDE

Planning Your Visit to Alton, Elsah and Grafton

For more information about the area, contact: Greater Alton/Twin Rivers Convention & Visitors Bureau (800/258-6645 or 618/465-6676).

Alton

The Alton Visitors Center at 200 Piasa St. is a good place to call ahead for information or to begin a tour of the town (800/258-6645).

LODGINGS

The Jackson House—Visitors may choose from three guest rooms in a historic 1880 home or a guest house that's a renovated horse barn. A hearty three-course breakfast includes homemade pie. Doubles from $75 (1821 Seminary St.; 800/462-1426 or 618/462-1426).

The Beall Mansion—Built in 1902, this 14-room, blond brick mansion at 407 E. 12th St. has been renovated into an elegant bed and breakfast with antique furnishings, Oriental rugs, marble and bronze statuary, and a hand-carved grand staircase. Four guest rooms are offered, each with two-person whirlpools. Doubles from $99 (800/990-BEAL or 618/474-9090).

DINING

The Franklin House—Located at 208 State St., the hotel where Abraham Lincoln stayed before his debate with Stephen Douglas in 1858 houses two garden tea rooms (618/463-1078) facing an English courtyard, as well as garden and gift shops (618/463-1050).

Cafe La Rose—Formerly the Alton Post Office, this building 300 Alby St. is the place for a quick lunch, including hearty soups, thick sandwiches and unforgettable desserts (618/463-2711).

Cane Bottom/My Just Desserts—Look out on the Mississippi while lunching on chicken salad or indulging in homemade desserts at 31 E. Broadway (618/462-5881).

SIGHTSEEING & RECREATION

Alton Museum of History and Art—Study Mississippi River memorabilia, as well as displays on town history. Look for the Robert Wadlow exhibit. Native-son Wadlow, who stood 8 feet 11 inches tall, is recognized as the tallest man in history. There's a life-size statue of the gentle giant on College Ave. (618/462-2763).

The Alton Antiques District—Head downtown to inspect several blocks of small shops and multidealer malls. These 19th-century buildings are located on and around Broadway, just a block from the river. For information, call 800/258-6645.

The Alton Belle Casino—A streamlined boat with Las Vegas-style decor, it holds 1,300 passengers and docks at the Alton riverfront. River cruises are scheduled every two hours from 7 a.m. to 3 p.m. (800/336-7568).

Gordon Moore Park—A 700-acre park along College Ave./Rte-140, offers picnic areas, hiking trails, a lake for fishing, playground equipment and an enchanting rose garden with more than 1,800 rose bushes (618/463-3580).

The Piasa Bird Painting—According to Indian legend, a monstrous bird patrolled the bluffs northwest of Alton, attacking those who violated its territory. The explorer Père Marquette noted paintings of the bird on his voyage here in 1673. Extensive quarrying in the 19th century destroyed the original paintings, but the legend lives on in this reproduction, which is undergoing repair until summer 1998. It is best seen from State-100 or from the river.

If visiting Alton in February and March, ask at the Alton Convention & Visitors Bureau about their wintertime guided tours of the Underground Railroad's local sites (800/258-6645).

FESTIVALS

The town of Godfrey, which adjoins Alton to the north, hosts Heritage Days each September. The festival includes historical reenactments and frontier crafts (618/465-4020).

home on the corner of LaSalle St. and Selma St. has five guest rooms, each with a private entrance. Perennial and rose gardens surround the house. Doubles from $80 (618/374-1684).

The Corner Nest Bed & Breakfast—A country look prevails at this 1883 French-American home on Elm St., with four guest rooms. Doubles from $70 (800/884-3832 or 618/374-1892).

Biking is one of many activities at Père Marquette State Park, located along the Great River Road.

In October, Alton honors its past with the Lincoln-Douglas Festival featuring crafts, an antiques show and food vendors (800/258-6645).

Elsah
LODGINGS

The Maple Leaf Cottage Inn—This 19th-century

The Green Tree Inn— This cheery red inn on Mill St. is a modern building constructed in the style of the 1850s. Each of the nine guest rooms is prettily decorated in a different motif. Doubles from $79 (618/374-2821).

Grafton
LODGINGS/DINING

Ruebel Hotel & Saloon— Overnight guests stay in 23 individually decorated rooms and suites. Doubles from $69. The Saloon restaurant is known for its fish basket meals (217 E. Main St., 618/786-2315).

The Tara Point Inn—A contemporary structure, this inn boasts a 200-foot-long deck overlooking the river. There are two guest rooms and one suite in the main house, and four suites in an adjoining cottage. The continental breakfast features home-baked pastries and fresh fruit. Doubles from $110 (618/786-3555).

Père Marquette State Park—Illinois' largest state park, found along the Great River Road, hosts numerous travelers drawn to its rustic stone-and-timber lodge built in the 1930s by the Civilian Conservation Corps and recently renovated. Choose one of 50 guest rooms in the lodge or stay in one of 22 individual cabins. Guests enjoy a full-service restaurant, an indoor pool, boating, fishing and horseback riding on 12 miles of trails. Doubles from $80 (618/786-2331).

The Fin Inn Restaurant— A traditional dish in river country, turtle soup is always on the menu. The dining room's three

oversize aquariums will fascinate children in this fun eatery along the Great River Road (618/786-2030).
The Brainerd House Bed and Breakfast—The popular Elsah Landing Restaurant and Bakery is now tucked in the Brainerd House Bed and Breakfast. You don't need to be a guest to enjoy its hearty soups, sand-wiches and great desserts (618/786-SOUP).

RECREATION
Raging Rivers Water Park—On the south edge of Grafton, there's family fun with a wave pool, water flumes and splash pools. It's open from June 15 through Labor Day (800/548-7573 or 618/786-2345).

SHOPPING
Old Rivertown Trading Company—This Main St. shop features folk art and garden accessories (618/786-2012).
Riverside Flea Market—From April through October, monthly flea markets take place in Grafton's historic Boatworks Building at 400 Front St. (618/462-8210).

FESTIVALS
In October, the Gathering of the Waters Rendezvous on Grafton's riverfront includes histor-ical reenactments of fron-tier life (618/786-3344).

OTHER PLACES TO VISIT IN THE AREA

Kampsville, Illinois
From Grafton, go north for 30 miles on State-100 to Kampsville, where the Center for American Archaeology directs area excavations of prehistoric Indian life. A visitors center in the former general store along State-100 in Kampsville includes exhibits about the ongoing research. The center also sponsors workshops, demonstra-tions, and field trips (618/653-4316).

Brussels, Illinois
The small town of Brussels, 10 miles west of Grafton, is home to the Wittmond Hotel, an 1847 stagecoach stop that houses an old-fashioned restaurant serving family-style meals (618/883-2345).

Hartford/Wood River, Illinois
The communities of Hartford and Wood River lie just south of Alton on State-3. During the winter of 1803-04, the famed Lewis and Clark expedition team camped here at the confluence of the Missouri and Mississippi rivers while making preparations for their epic journey to the Pacific coast. The Lewis and Clark Historic Site, just south of Hartford off of State-3, includes a monument consisting of 11 concrete pylons—one for each state traversed by the expedition.
Wood River is the site of an Aquatic Center with two water slides, an Olympic-size pool, and wading and diving areas. Open Memorial Day through mid-September (618/251-3130).

Cahokia Mounds State Historic Site, Illinois
For a glimpse of life along the Mississippi River long before the arrival of the Europeans, visit Cahokia Mounds

ILLINOIS BUREAU OF TOURISM

Native Americans celebrate Heritage America, a fall festival at Cahokia Mounds.

State Historic Site, 25 miles south of Alton (take exit 24 off of I-255). The fascinating 2,200-acre site contains the remains of an ancient city that was the most sophisticated prehistoric Indian civilization north of Mexico.

The United Nations has recognized its cultural and historical importance, designating it a World Heritage Site, one of only 500 such places in the world.

An ancient society of 10,000 to 20,000 people inhabited Cahokia from about 700 A.D. to 1500 A.D. Houses were arranged in rows around open plazas, and the many mounds may have served as bases for ceremonial buildings and chiefs' houses, as well as burial grounds.

At Cahokia Mounds, you'll see 68 of more than 100 earthen mounds, plus the reconstruction of one of four circular sun calendars. Monks Mound, named for the Trappist monastery that once existed nearby, has a base that covers over 14 acres. Rising to a height of 100 feet, it's the largest prehistoric earthen construction in the New World. A trail marked with information leads visitors to its summit.

Before you wander the site, see the 33,000-square-foot museum and interpretive center, which is open daily. Its displays will help you understand the complex culture that once flourished here. For information, contact: Cahokia Mounds State Historic Site, 30 Ramey St., Collinsville, IL 62234 (618/346-5160).

Cahokia, Illinois

The city of Cahokia, 30 miles south of Alton, takes pride in two historic sites. The Cahokia Courthouse State Historic Site at First and Elm streets preserves a structure believed to be the oldest in the state. Built in 1737, it served as the political center for the immense Northwest Territory until 1814 (618/332-1782).

Another Cahokia landmark is the 1799 Holy Family Log Church, the oldest French log church in Illinois still in continuous use. Its construction is unusual. The walnut logs stand vertically, instead of being stacked horizontally. The cemetery behind the church also will be of interest. The National Historic Landmark is at First St. and Church St. (618/332-4548).

Belleville, Illinois

Thirty-five miles to the south of Alton lies the city of Belleville, which in the early 1800s was an important political and manufacturing center for southern Illinois. Tours of the historic homes and churches in the city's downtown are offered through the Belleville Tourism Office (800/677-9255 or 618/233-6769).

The National Shrine of Our Lady of the Snows sits atop a bluff in Belleville. The 200-acre site, dedicated to Mary, is the largest outdoor shrine in the United States. It includes a replica of the grotto at Lourdes, France. Each Christmas, the shrine displays nearly a million white lights. Located along State-15 at 442 S. DeMazenod Dr., the site includes a gift shop, gardens, amphitheater, restaurant and motel (618/397-6700).

Belleville is also the site of the 1,200-seat Cathedral of Saint Peter, the largest structure of its kind in Illinois. The 1852 Gothic church at 200 W. Harrison is modeled after England's Exeter Cathedral.

Another Belleville attraction is Eckert's Country Store and Farms, one of the largest pick-your-own orchards in the nation. Stroll the fruit orchards, take a wagon tour and enjoy petting the animals. Special events and festivals are held year-round. The farms are along State-15 E. and Greenmount Rd. (618/233-0513).

By Lori Erickson

DOWN RIVER

French fur traders who pitted their vulnerable canoes against the treacherous sandbars and unpredictable currents of the Mississippi River 300 years ago discovered a land teeming with wildlife and soil rich with the river's deposits. French settlements quickly followed, flourishing along the riverbanks and building a powerful legacy in the Heartland.

The modest village of St. Louis became a jumping-off point for pioneers headed west and a magnet for ambitious immigrants who built breweries, shoe factories and fortunes. The city wears its French heritage lightly, mainly in place names such as Lafayette Square, Soulard, and Laclede's Landing.

The Mississippi River's French accent becomes more pronounced as you head south to Ste. Genevieve, the site of dozens of French colonial buildings that predate the American Revolution. You'll uncover more French history in Missouri towns such as Cape Girardeau and in Illinois' Prairie Du Rocher.

Other countries left their imprint, too. The town of New Madrid recalls Spain's claims to North American territories in the 1700s. German immigrants fleeing political instability for the promise of unlimited opportunity in the New World established Altenburg and Wittenberg, Missouri.

In southern Illinois, the towns of Thebes and Cairo acquired their exotic names as a tribute to the cities along Egypt's Nile River delta. Little Cairo, perched on bluffs that overlook the spot where the Mississippi and Ohio Rivers join, was a vital Union Army outpost during the Civil War.

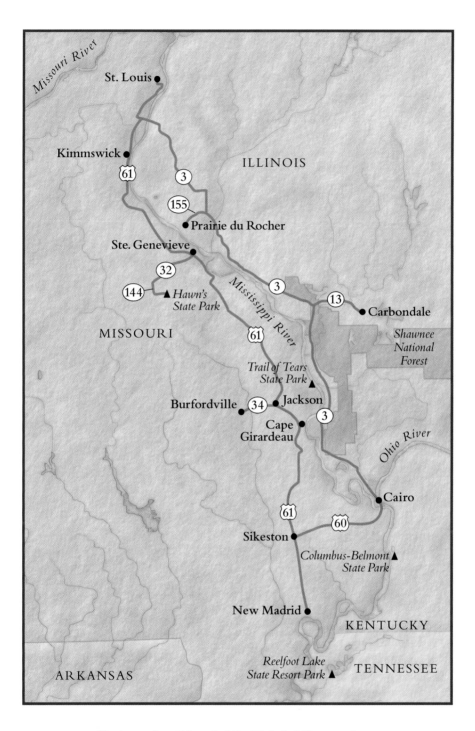

The towns along this part of the Mississippi River acquire
a hint of Dixie, a reminder that the heritage of the Midwest
is an amalgam of many histories, legends, and cultures,
each unique and significant.

ST. LOUIS

The Gateway to the West serves up good food and good music with a dollop of history.

Soulard, The Hill, The Loop—St. Louis is a city of neighborhoods, all fanning out from a broad, brawny riverfront and the shining, soaring arch where all first-time visitors should start their sojourn.

Looking at Gateway City

For the best view of the riverfront, head right to the top of the stairs at the base of the 630-foot stainless-steel Gateway Arch. The arch, America's tallest national monument (it's 75 feet taller than the Washington Monument), symbolizes the city's role as the starting point of our country's western expansion. Two bridges frame the river view here: on the right, the modern Poplar Street Bridge, and on the left, the grimy stone towers and jet-black steel trusses of the 1874 Eads Bridge, an engineering masterpiece.

Below, you'll see the cobblestone landing— called a levee here—littered with the small rocks and pieces of flotsam that children gleefully throw into the water, just as they did when steamboats moored to unload their cargo. But with the exception of the *Becky Thatcher* and *Tom Sawyer* excursion boats, today's riverfront tenants— the Admiral casino boat and McDonald's restaurant boat—are moored permanently.

Take the tram ride to the top of the arch for glorious views of the city of St. Louis, then head out to explore its riches at ground level.

Laclede's Landing And Soulard

Laclede's Landing, born when Frenchman Pierre Laclede set up a trading post in 1764, is a city of aged, renovated brick buildings along the narrow, cobblestone streets just north of the Gateway Arch. In this area, it's easy to imagine the St. Louis riverfront district when the port was a clamorous hub of steamboat commerce. Many of the old warehouses sport ornate facades with intricate brick work and unique stone cornices. They once stored everything from butter churns and wagon wheels for settlers headed west to tanned hides and furs destined for fashionable consumers back East. Today,

The Gateway Arch soars above the city and the river.

the area bustles with visitors and local folk visiting restaurants, shops and bars. This is the place to hear live music, from alternative rock and mainstream pop to jazz and St. Louis' own sweet soul music, the blues and ragtime.

South of downtown is Soulard, a neighborhood of brick sidewalks anchored by an outdoor farmers market dating to 1779. Residents who like the urban coziness of ornately decorated red brick row houses rediscovered Soulard. Wrought-iron balconies and fences, as well as the occasional arched brick walkway between buildings, reflect a strong French influence. The community's French roots surface each February during Soulard Mardi Gras, a smaller yet enthusiastic version of the tumultuous event in New Orleans.

Soulard's bars and restaurants include McGurk's, an authentic Irish pub with plenty of beer, arguably the best burgers in the city and Irish musicians who render the rollicking and poignant tunes of their homeland. Always lively with American flavor is Mike & Min's, which serves up pork, chicken and steaks, plus big helpings of the blues.

Heading West

West of downtown, Forest Park sprawls across 1,200 acres. Explore the St. Louis Art Museum, History Museum, St. Louis Zoo and St. Louis Science Center's Planetarium in this vast green space. The art museum and zoo buildings are among the few permanent reminders of the colossal 1904 World's Fair, believed by some to be the greatest moment in St. Louis history. All of the attractions here are free, and you pay just $1 to ride from one to another all day on the brightly painted Shuttle Bug.

On the way to Forest Park, you may want to detour for a drive through two interesting residential areas southwest of downtown. Lafayette Park is the fulcrum of the Lafayette Square neighborhood, a nationally renowned collection of Victorian residences, several of which are now bed and breakfasts.

A few blocks south and west of Lafayette Square in Compton Heights are Longfellow and Hawthorne streets, with their late-19th-century mansions, many built by the city's beer barons. These turreted and gabled homes constructed of

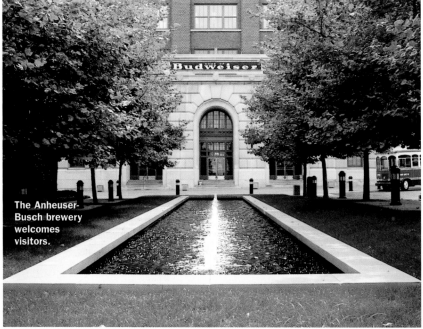

The Anheuser-Busch brewery welcomes visitors.

A Mardi Gras parade celebrates Soulard's French roots.

white and red stone and bricks are reminiscent of English country estates and French châteaux.

The Hill— St. Louis' Little Italy

Compton Heights' beer barons were on the opposite end of the social spectrum from the working-class Italians who built the neat rows of bungalows in The Hill neighborhood at Kingshighway and Shaw Avenue. Accompanied by well-maintained, postage-stamp-size lawns, the homes line narrow streets. You'll recognize Little Italy on seeing fire hydrants painted the red, green and white colors of the Italian flag.

But The Hill isn't here just for looks. Where enticing aromas waft, delicacies abound. Italian cuisine reigns supreme, from the casual atmosphere of Rigazzi's, where patrons down frozen fishbowls of beer and toasted ravioli appetizers—a St. Louis invention—to the more formal ambience of candle-lit Giovanni's. Italian sub sandwiches are a staple at several delis and food stores, most notably at Amighetti's Bakery, where the bread draws crowds, and at specialty stores such as John Viviano & Sons Grocery Co. Do-it-yourselfers can put together their own lunch with thinly sliced, spicy Genoa salami from John Volpe & Co. and a fresh-baked, aromatic loaf of Italian bread, followed by cannoli filled with ricotta cream cheese or custard from Missouri Baking Co. For a great cook-at-home meal, pick up authentic ravioli at Mama Toscano's Market.

Central West End And The Loop

A cosmopolitan atmosphere pervades two midtown neighborhoods where curbside tables at cafes and bars encourage people-watching. In the upscale Central West End, antiques shops, art galleries and restaurants are interspersed among stately homes.

Northwest of Forest Park in University City, The Loop is a lively strip of bars, ethnic restaurants and specialty shops along Delmar Boulevard. In The Loop, babyboomers crowd Cicero's, a restaurant and bar with 47 draft and 105 bottled brands of beer. Blueberry Hill serves 18 beers on tap and 100 bottled brands, while the jukebox blares rock.

Before you leave The Loop, stroll the St. Louis Walk of Fame. Bronze stars embedded in the sidewalks on both sides of Delmar honor hometown notables from Scott Joplin to Chuck Berry.

Planning Your Visit to St. Louis

For information about attractions, lodgings and more stop at the St. Louis Visitor Information Center, 701 Convention Plaza (800/916-0092).

It's easy to get around St. Louis on Metrolink, the light transit railway that runs from East St. Louis to Lambert St. Louis International Airport, with stops near many of the attractions listed here (314/231-2345).

LODGINGS

Omni Hotel Majestic—A comfortable European-style hotel, this downtown landmark has 91 luxurious rooms, marble baths and a cozy restaurant and lounge. Doubles from $115 (314/436-2355).

Ritz-Carlton—Antiques, art, fresh flowers, after-noon tea and soothing classical music in the lobby make this hotel in Clayton worth the 10-minute drive from downtown. Doubles from $225 (800/241-3333).

Adam's Mark Hotel— This hotel's 910 rooms and views of the Gateway Arch are accented by elegant common areas and indoor and outdoor pools. Doubles from $189 (800/483-2666).

Lafayette House Bed and Breakfast—Of six com-fortably decorated rooms, three offer private baths. All guests enjoy a gourmet breakfast in this lovingly restored Victorian home near downtown. The house overlooks Lafayette Park, amid one of the areas most noted for Victorian architecture in the U.S. Doubles from $60 (800/641-8965 or 314/772-4429).

Preston Place—Two clean, uncluttered rooms with private baths (one adjoining), antiques, high ceilings and full breakfast enhance this Victorian treasure at 1835 Lafayette Ave., just minutes from downtown. Doubles from $75 (314/664-3429).

Hyatt Regency—This 540-room hotel shares the magnificently restored Union Station with nearly 100 shops and restaurants, and is on the Metrolink line. Doubles from $205 (800/233-1234).

Lemp Mansion Restaurant and Inn— The adventurous may opt to overnight in this supposedly haunted Victorian mansion, which claims three on-site suicides by members of the beer-brewing dynasty that once owned it. The mansion has two time-worn but spacious rooms, two suites, and ornate mantels and vintage fixtures through-out. Doubles from $85 (314/664-8024).

DINING

O'Connell's Pub—In a dead heat with McGurk's for the best burgers in town, this casual pub at Kingshighway and Shaw is perfect for grabbing a sandwich, fries and a cold one (314/773-6600).

Rigazzi's—For four decades, this eatery on The Hill has served ravioli and affordable platters of pasta. The boisterous setting features 32-ounce "frozen" fishbowls of beer (314/772-4900).

Tony's—As fine as dining gets in St. Louis, Tony's impeccable service and specialties such as lobster albanello and linguini with clams have earned this elegant downtown eatery superior ratings (314/231-7007).

Blueberry Hill Restaurant and Pub—Beer, sand-wiches, darts and a juke-box of rock-'n'-roll greats make this Loop stop a St. Louis landmark (314/727-0880).

Cicero's—The town's largest selection of draft beer, good food and rock 'n' roll liven this Loop staple (314/862-0009).

Balaban's—This elegant Central West End restaurant's specialties include mesquite-grilled swordfish and roast duck (314/361-8085).

Ted Drewes Frozen Custard—Imagine "concrete" shakes so thick they're served upside down—many say it's the best custard in the world. Find this longtime local favorite at 6726 Chippewa St. (314/481-2652). Kemoll's—Fine dining is the rule at this dressy family-run Italian restaurant featuring a range of pastas such as fettuccini with smoked salmon and a variety of veal and meat favorites. The restaurant is located in downtown St. Louis' tallest building (314/421-0555).

Russell St. in the historic Soulard neighborhood (314/776-8309). Riddle's Penultimate Cafe and Wine Bar— Delicious daily specialties range from seafood to meat dishes, plus homemade ice cream. This establishment, located along Delmar in The Loop, serves more than 350 kinds of wine so allow enough time to select and quaff your favorite vintage (314/725-6985).

Co. (314/772-8550); Italian groceries at John Viviano & Sons Grocery Co. (314/771-5476); fresh-baked goods including bread and cookies at Missouri Baking Co. (314/773-6566); and unsurpassed ravioli at Mama Toscano's Market (314/776-2926).

ENTERTAINMENT

Look for live music north of the Gateway Arch in Laclede's Landing, a bustling district with cobblestone streets and renovated 19th-century buildings that is south of downtown near the historic Soulard neighborhood. The bars are interspersed among homes dating from the mid-1800s. Bars sought out by jazz and blues enthusiasts include the Broadway Oyster Bar (314/621-8811) just south of downtown; Laffite's (314/241-5722) on The Landing; Faust's (314/241-7400) in the Adam's Mark Hotel downtown; Mike & Min's (314/421-1655) in Soulard; and Off Broadway (314/773-3363) in south St. Louis. A comprehensive listing of St. Louis bands by type and venue is printed in the Get Out section of the *St. Louis Post-Dispatch* each Thursday. The Muny—See locally produced and touring musicals at the largest

ST. LOUIS CONVENTION & VISITORS COMMISSION

The History Museum, one of several outstanding cultural institutions clustered in Forest Park.

John D. McGurk's Irish Pub—Expect elaborate burgers, beer and beautiful Irish music, usually played by musicians from the Emerald Isle. The pub is found south of downtown at 1200

Food is king on The Hill in various restaurants and eateries: Italian cuisine at Giovanni's (314/772-5958); specialty subs at Amighetti's Bakery (314/776-2855); Italian salami at John Volpe &

outdoor amphitheater in the country. The shows, booked throughout the summer, have become a St. Louis tradition (314/361-1900).

Fabulous Fox Theater— This renovated and outrageously decorated movie palace at 527 N. Grand Blvd. is a venue for Broadway-style shows and other entertainment and can be toured for a small fee (314/534-1678).

St. Louis Symphony— Performing in magnificent Powell Hall, two blocks north of the Fox, the orchestra has won several Grammy Awards and the hearts of European audiences (314/534-1700).

President Casino on the Admiral—The first riverboat casino in Missouri is permanently moored on the riverfront (314/622-1111).

SIGHTSEEING

The Gateway Arch— Soaring ever upward from the Jefferson National Expansion Memorial, a federal park along the St. Louis riverfront, the tallest national monument offers a tram ride to its 630-foot summit. A magnificent view of the St. Louis area and nearby Illinois can reach 30 miles on a clear day. There's a film on the building of the arch that you won't want to miss and an IMAX Theater that offers two different

films (314/425-6010).

The Old Courthouse— The city's transition from fur-trading center to springboard for westward expansion is chronicled here in exhibits that include the Dred Scott decision, a famous slavery case that helped precipitate the Civil War (314/425-6010).

Cathedral Basilica of St. Louis—The largest collection of mosaic art in the world decorates the interior of this church at 4431 Lindell Blvd. in midtown. A pocket museum on the lower level explains how the art was created (314/533-0544).

The Missouri Botanical Garden—This 79-acre treasure at 4344 Shaw Blvd. has a tropical rain forest under a geodesic dome called the Climatron, an enchanting Japanese Garden with giant koi and graceful bridges, a Victorian maze with viewing cupola and more than 20 demonstration home gardens (314/577-5100).

Anheuser-Busch Brewery Tour Center—A tour of the historic brewery at 12th and Lynch includes stops at the Clydesdale stables and a bottling facility, a brief video on the making of beer, a short ride on a cable car and complimentary samples of beer and soft drinks. All is free, but reservations are required

for groups of 15 or more (314/577-2626).

Gateway Riverboat Cruises—Two paddle wheelers cruise daily from beneath the Gateway Arch from April to September, weather and river conditions permitting (314/621-4040).

Soulard Market— Operating since 1779, this farmers market just

ST. LOUIS CONVENTION & VISITORS COMMISSION

At the Missouri Botanical Garden, savor woodland, scented and traditional Japanese gardens.

south of downtown has about 150 stalls selling fresh fruit and many other items Wednesdays through Saturdays (314/622-4180).

SHOPPING

Union Station—Once the busiest train station in the world, this painstakingly renovated Richardsonian Romanesque structure at Market St. and 18th St. is a mustsee for architecture buffs. It now houses the Hyatt Regency, a luxury hotel with a breathtaking lobby bar that once was the station's soaring Grand Hall. The depot also encloses a collection of sit-down restaurants, a food court and family-oriented shops and carts that include The Great Train Store, The Nature Store and The Disney Store. Free concerts are given during the summer (314/421-6655). The Saint Louis Galleria— Visitors find the finest upscale shopping west of downtown at I-64 (US-40) and Brentwood Blvd. (314/863-6633).

MUSEUMS

Forest Park—Found at Kingshighway and I-64 (US-40), Forest Park's 1,200 acres are home to a gathering of cultural institutions, along with a scenic 7½-mile hiking and biking trail, fishing, golf, tennis and picnic facilities. During the summer, the Forest Park Shuttle Bug stops at all the park museums. Board it at the Forest Park or Central West End Metrolink stations or at one of the marked bus stops in the park (314/231-2345). The institutions, all free, include: the St. Louis Art Museum (314/721-0072), with Oriental collections, decorative arts and paintings; the History Museum (314/361-9265), with an array of exhibits, from information about fur

traders who founded the city to African-American musicians who helped give it a musical identity; the St. Louis Zoo (314/781-0900), 90 acres, including world-class exhibits housing more than 3,600 animals and the largest free-flight aviary in the world; and the St. Louis Science Center (314/289-4444), with more than 500 interactive and hands-on exhibits, a Planetarium and an Omnimax theater. Laumeier Sculpture Park—Just 30 minutes from downtown, works of art stand along-side hiking trails on more than 96 acres and a small museum houses indoor art exhibits (314/821-1209). Museum of Westward Expansion—Found below the Gateway Arch, this museum uses artifacts, authentic photographs and fascinating exhibits to tell the story of westward expansion (314/425-6010). City Museum—St. Louis artist Robert J. Cassilly weds art and recycled materials in a former shoe warehouse at 701 N. 15th St. (314/231-2489). International Bowling Museum & St. Louis Cardinals Hall of Fame— Exhibits review more than a century of sports at 111 Stadium St. (314/231-6340). Scott Joplin House— Memorabilia fills the

home of this composer at 2658 Delmar Blvd. (314/533-1003). Soldiers' Memorial Military Museum—Free and open to the public, the museum, located at 1315 Chestnut St., displays items from the Civil War and both world wars (314/622-4550). Eugene Field House and St. Louis Toy Museum— The home of the children's poet at 634 S. Broadway showcases antique toys and dolls (314/421-4689).

FESTIVALS

Fair Saint Louis—One of the nation's largest birthday parties, this July Fourth event on the Gateway Arch grounds includes a kick-off parade, concerts by national entertainers, elaborate air shows, activity booths, ethnic foods, various small stages and spectacular fireworks displays (314/434-3434). Japanese Festival—This Labor Day weekend staple at the Missouri Botanical Garden offers musical performances, cultural demonstrations, vendors of Japanese products and an unforgettable night walk through the Japanese Garden, with hundreds of lanterns lining the paths and floating on the water (314/577-5100).

By Randy Cosby

STE. GENEVIEVE

The Heartland's French legacy lives on in the homes and shops of Missouri's oldest town.

Slow your car as you descend Market Street into the heart of Ste. Genevieve (population: 4,400), and history will envelope you. Here, 60 miles south of St. Louis, is the oldest permanent settlement west of the Mississippi River. Founded in 1735, the town, an architectural treasure, boasts the best collection of French Creole buildings in the U.S.

In this working community, many historic buildings still are in use as homes or businesses. The telltale signs of "progress" such as cubelike glass-and-brick buildings, parking lots and convenience stores rarely exist. Stop at the tourist information center along Main Street to view a 15-minute video about the town's history and to pick up a walking-tour map. Then, you're ready to stroll the streets of downtown Ste. Genevieve.

Exploring the Past

Decades before Meriwether Lewis and William Clark set off on their momentous 1803-06 journey to explore the lands west of the Mississippi, French settlers built their homes here. It's difficult to walk a block or turn a corner without seeing a building bearing a plaque that dates it to the late 1700s or early 1800s.

The oldest brick building west of the Mississippi, at Market and Third streets, anchors one corner of Dubourg Square. Dating from the mid-1700s, the two-story, red-roofed structure of handmade bricks now houses the aptly named Old Brick House restaurant. Fried chicken and home-style mashed potatoes share the menu with *knaeflies*, luscious little liver dumplings, a culinary contribution of Ste. Genevieve's early German settlers.

A half block farther stands the Southern Hotel, a classic Federal-style building with a dormered roof and a broad front porch. Constructed in 1805, it won fame for having the first pool table west of the Mississippi. Today, it's been skillfully renovated as a bed and breakfast and decorated whimsically with a unique collection of country Victorian antiques. Be sure to see the old summer kitchen behind the hotel. Built to keep the heat of cooking and laundry chores away from the main house, the Southern Hotel's kitchen houses a shop with

BILL ENGEL/PHOTOGRAPHIC RESOURCES, INC.

The oldest brick building west of the Mississippi.

collectibles and garden accessories.

Across the square is the Ste. Genevieve Museum. It displays an assortment of artifacts and documents chronicling the tale of the enterprising French farmers, traders and lead miners who founded the village and the German immigrants who followed.

Architecture Buffs, Rejoice!

Ste. Genevieve claims astounding examples of late-18th-century French colonial architecture. Nearly 40 buildings showcase the signature traits of French Creole construction: upright logs, steep hip roofs supported by enormous Norman trusses and wide galleries (or porches) skirting the structures. All but three of these log buildings were constructed in the *poteaux-sur-solle* style, meaning the logs are set on a stone foundation.

The three exceptions are built in the *poteaux-en-terre* style, with the hand-hewn logs set directly in the ground. Only two other examples are found in the U.S. Cedar logs, practically indestructible, contribute to the longevity of *poteaux en terre*.

State-owned and operated Amoureux

House represents an excellent example of this nearly extinct style of construction. Built in 1770 on St. Mary's Road, it overlooks Le Grand Champ ("the big field"), the shared farming area situated between the river and the early settlers' homes.

Bolduc House, circa 1770, best illustrates log-on-stone construction. In fact, it's probably one of the finest examples of French colonial construction in the U.S. It's easy to understand how much effort the original owner, Louis Bolduc, a prosperous merchant, lead miner and farmer, exerted to build this home in the New World wilderness.

Authentic furnishings enhance the finely restored structure enclosed by a stockade fence of upright logs. The simple interior has two plank-floored rooms: a large open area where most of the family activity took place and a small bedroom separated from the main room by a hallway with an entrance to the loft. The original kitchen is behind the house. The lovingly tended medicinal herb gardens and grape arbor thrive nearby.

The Felix Valle State Historic Site is located a few blocks from Bolduc House. Merchant Jacob Philipson built

In costume at French Fort du Chartres (see page 124).

BARBARA MARTIN

Bolduc House, a fine example of French colonial architecture.

FRANK OBERLE

the limestone story-and-a-half home in 1818. Later bought by prominent merchant Felix Valle, the home, which once had an adjacent store, shows the increasing sophistication of affluent Ste. Genevieve residents.

Unlike the central family room in the Bolduc House, these interiors partition into high-ceilinged rooms with specific purposes. The presence of early French Empire furnishings and ready-made clothes shows the impact of the steamboats, which started bringing freight upriver from New Orleans the year after the house was built.

Present-Day Pleasures Downtown

Ste. Genevieve is more than an intriguing time capsule. Along with tours of a half-dozen historic homes, a splendid church and a historic cemetery, the venerable downtown district highlights restaurants serving home-cooked regional favorites.

Visitors especially enjoy one-of-a-kind shops with antiques, arts and crafts.

Browse in Odile's Linens & Lace to see a quaint collection of lace collars, dresser scarves and other exquisite textiles. A vintage barber shop is the unusual setting.

Allow time for refreshments during this pleasant interlude. Sara's Ice Cream and Antiques is the place to quench even the fiercest thirst on hot afternoons. Satisfy lunchtime appetites with a burger at the historic Anvil Saloon and Restaurant.

Bed-and-breakfast inns in or near downtown accommodate a wide range of tastes. Along with the Southern Hotel, you can choose from traditionally styled rooms and suites in the Inn St. Gemme Beauvais— Missouri's oldest continuously operating bed and breakfast—or the spare yet elegant accommodations at the Main Street Inn. An overnight stay in a venerable old inn is sure to make you a part of Ste. Genevieve history.

Planning Your Visit to Ste. Genevieve

For more information, contact: Ste. Genevieve Tourist Information Office (573/883-7097).

LODGINGS

Motels include the Family Budget Inn (573/543-2272), a few miles from town along I-55 at Ozora exit 143; two smaller motels are located along US-61, about 5 miles from town.

The Hotel Sainte Genevieve—These squeaky-clean basic rooms are found at Main and Merchant streets downtown. Doubles from $45 (573/543-2272).

Main Street Inn Bed and Breakfast—This three-story brick building with 11½-foot-high ceilings possesses a magnificent kitchen, game room and eight elegant but simply-furnished guest rooms. Doubles from $65 (800/918-9199).

Inn Ste. Gemme Beauvais—Missouri's oldest continuously operated bed and break-fast, the mid-1800s brick inn is known for high ceilings, elaborate woodwork and a well-tended garden. The hosts graciously serve high tea and wine. Eight guest rooms and suites are available. Doubles from $89, including breakfast in Cafe Frances (800/818-5744).

Southern Hotel Bed and Breakfast—A beautifully restored 1805 Federal building, this bed and breakfast includes eight romantic guest rooms decorated with Victorian country antiques. Doubles from $80 (800/275-1412).

Somewhere Inn Time Bed and Breakfast—The two-story colonial home has won awards for its interior design. A swimming pool, four guest rooms with vintage furnishings, whirlpool tubs and one cottage beside the oudoor pool add to the ambience. Doubles from $95 (573/883-9397 or toll-free in Missouri and Illinois, 888/883-9397).

Creole House Bed and Breakfast—This modern residence on St. Mary's Rd. tastefully blends in with nearby French Creole structures. Two suites, two bedrooms and an open floor plan featuring a spacious sitting room with fireplace contribute to the charm. Doubles from $85 (800/275-6041).

DINING

Anvil Saloon & Restaurant—Claiming the best onion rings west of the Mississippi, Anvil's also wins praise for burgers, liver dumplings and homemade pies. Found on the square at S. Third St., the building dates to the 1850s

(573/883-2323).

Old Brick House—Choose from crispy fried chicken with homemade mashed potatoes, liver dumplings, a buffet or a sirloin steak in the oldest brick building west of the Mississippi. The restaurant is located on the square at Third St. and Market St. (573/883-2724).

Cafe Frances in the Inn Ste. Gemme Beauvais—A savory French onion soup stands out among the light French fare served daily except Wednesdays in this lovely tea room setting (573/883-5744).

Sirros—Locals flock to 261 Merchant St. for pasta, cheeseburgers and spicy french fries (573/883-5749).

Winds of Meadowview—Affordable dining with a French accent is served in an elegant château set in the Missouri countryside along Rte. B about 12 miles south of Ste. Genevieve (573/883-9940).

Hotel Ste. Genevieve—The restaurant menu includes excellent steaks, chicken and seafood (573/883-3562).

Kmetz Home Bakery—Fresh-baked cookies, bread and other treats are offered daily at this Merchant St. favorite (573/883-3533).

Jack Oberle Market—About ½ mile west of downtown on State-32,

Jack follows his great-grandfather's recipe for hickory-smoked all-beef sausage that locals lovingly call the Oberle "dog." Other favorites include smoked pork loin and garlic cheese (573/883-5656).

Sara's Ice Cream & Antiques—Hand-dipped ice cream, phosphates, delicious homemade drumsticks and ice cream sodas provide a refreshing break along downtown's Merchant St. (573/883-5853).

DAVID ULMER/PHOTOGRAPHIC RESOURCES, INC.

The rustic rockers on the broad front porch of Ste. Genevieve's Southern Hotel invite visitors to relax.

SIGHTSEEING

Bolduc House—This outstanding example of French colonial archi-tecture was built south of town in 1770 by trader and miner Louis Bolduc, then moved away from the river in 1784. Notable features include a stockade fence, hip roof, galleries, medicinal herb gardens, grape arbor and authentic furnishings from the period (573/883-3105).

Bolduc-LeMeilleur House—The brace-frame structure with brick nog-ging shows how French and American influences began to mix by 1820, when Bolduc's grandson-in-law built the house. It's furnished with early Federal pieces, while herb and scented gardens flourish nearby (573/883-3105).

Felix Valle State Historic Site—This 1818 Georgian-colonial-style building still has original mantels and interior trim, as well as brick and frame outbuildings in its garden and orchard. The state also restored the Shaw House, a neighboring structure with an 1830s kitchen (573/883-7102).

Amoureux House—The *poteaux-en-terre* (posts in the ground) method of setting log walls upright in the earth was well known when this house was built in 1792, although only five such structures now exist, three of them in Ste. Genevieve. The state owns and operates the historic

home along St. Mary's Rd., which overlooks Le Grand Champ agricultural fields (573/883-7102).

Maison Guibourd-Valle House—The tastefully furnished 1784 home features costumed guides, changing exhibits and dried herb displays in an attic featuring an incredible Norman truss and hand-hewn oak beams secured by wooden pegs. The courtyard contains an old stone well and rose garden (573/883-7544).

Hawn's State Park—Avid hikers and backpackers can explore the breathtaking scenery along the Whispering Pine or Pickle Creek trails. Many stop for lunch at one of several picnic sites in the park at State-32 and State-144 (573/883-3603).

SHOPPING

Surrounded by buildings listed in the National Register of Historic Places, more than two dozen shops downtown offer antiques, art, crafts and collectibles.

Al Agnew Gallery—Animals are the subjects of the works displayed at 10 S. Main St.

Summer Kitchen—This shop behind the South-ern Hotel brims with collectibles and garden accessories. Antiques-hunters' delights include: Odile's Vintage

Lace & Linens, 34 S. Third St.; The Mill Antique Mart, 305 N. Main St.; and La Galerie of the French Quarter, 305 Merchant St.
Show Me Shop—Find gifts galore at 73 N. Main St., where you can buy wine, cheese, sausage and other foods produced in Missouri (573/883-3096).

FESTIVALS
Bastille Day—Visitors snap photos with "Madame Guillotine," indulge in French food and movies, and take candlelight tours through the historic sections of town in mid-July (573/883-7097).
Jour de Fête—Arts, crafts, antiques, street performers and music flood the historic downtown each mid-August. Actors, dressed in authentic costumes, reenact French frontier life (573/883-7097).
Country Christmas Walk—Mr. and Mrs. Santa Claus, carolers and a live nativity scene complement a town dressed in period Christmas decorations in early December (573/883-7097).

MUSEUMS
Ste. Genevieve Museum—Built during the town's Bicentennial in 1935, the museum contains artifacts and memorabilia from the native mound-building Indians, old documents and Spanish land grants, antique weapons and artifacts from the state's first industry, the Saline Creek Salt Works (573/883-3461).

CAMPING
Hawn's State Park— Fifty campsites (26 with electrical hookups) are available on a first-come, first-served basis in the park at State-32 and State-144. Amenities include modern restrooms, hot showers (water off from November 1 to April 1), laundry facilities and playground equipment (573/883-3603).

The Pierre Menard Home was once owned by Illinois' first lieutenant governor (see page 125).

OTHER PLACES TO VISIT IN THE AREA
Historic French colonial sites abound on both sides of the Mississippi. About 10 miles south is Kaskaskia Island, where a shrine houses the 650-pound bronze-and-silver Liberty Bell of the West, a gift from the King of France to French settlers in the 1700s.
Visitors also can take the Ste. Genevieve Modoc Ferry from Little Rock Landing just north of Ste. Genevieve to the Illinois side of the river, where State-3 leads to several remarkable French frontier sites.
Fort de Chartres State Historic Site, with an impressive partially restored stone fort dating to the early 18th century, is about 4 miles west of Illinois' oldest town, Prairie Du Rocher, along State-155 (618/284-7230). The northern approach from the parking lot to the fort is breath-taking, with 15-foot walls protected at the corners by even taller bastions and accented in the center by a towering gatehouse. Inside are reconstructed barracks, a museum and a restored powder magazine that is the

only surviving structure from the original fort.

In early June, the Fort de Chartres Trappers and Traders Rendezvous brings military and civilian reenactors who set up camp and present authentic cooking, crafts making, dancing and other activities from the French colonial period (618/284-7230).

South along State-3 is the Pierre Menard Home, residence of Illinois' first lieutenant governor and a notable example of French colonial architecture (618/859-3031). Nearby, the Fort Kaskaskia Historic Site preserves remnants of another early fort.

DINING & LODGINGS

La Maison du Rocher Country Inn Bed and Breakfast—Stay overnight in Prairie du Rocher and enjoy homemade pies, breads, jellies, jams, country cooking and suites with private baths. Doubles from $55 (618/284-3463).

Kimmswick

Kimmswick, about 38 miles north of Ste. Genevieve, was founded in 1859 by Theodore Kimm, a native of Brunswick, Germany, who chose the site because of its proximity to the river and a rail line. Many of the 19th-century brick buildings have been restored. The four-square-block downtown area boasts restaurants, two bed and breakfasts and a unique sampling of crafts, collectibles, arts and antiques shops. (All shops close on Monday, and many of the historic buildings are open only during festivals.) For more information, contact: Kimmswick Tourist Information Office (314/464-6464).

LODGINGS

Chain motels abound along I-55. Wenom-Drake House Bread and Breakfast—A beautiful two-story frame home with three guest rooms, the bed and breakfast is furnished with antiques. View the village and surrounding area from its perch atop a hill overlooking downtown. The hearty breakfasts include grits. Doubles from $50 (314/464-1983).

Kimmswick Korner Inn Bed and Breakfast—This two-story brick building along Front St. has two comfortably decorated and airy guest rooms on the second floor (shared bath and entrance from the parlor). Breakfast includes homemade cinnamon rolls, bread, cheeses, fruit, jellies and jams. Doubles from $60 (314/467-1028).

DINING

The Blue Owl Restaurant & Bakery— A 19th-century structure known as The Tavern houses the Blue Owl. Stop for a big breakfast or hearty lunch and enjoy generous helpings of homemade food and fabulous desserts Tuesdays through Sundays (314/464-3128).

Old House Restaurant— Immense overhead beams and plank flooring impress diners in this magnificently renovated two-story 18th-century log cabin. Lunch and dinner specialties include prime rib, chicken and dumplings and homemade desserts Tuesdays through Sundays (314/464-0378).

FESTIVALS

Kimmswick Days Festival—Crafts demonstrations, along with more than 100 booths and exhibits, occur each mid-May (314/464-6464).

Christmas Candlelight Tour—The village and several historic and private homes, all decorated in full holiday regalia open their doors to the public the first weekend in December (314/464-6464).

By Jane Cosby

CAPE GIRARDEAU

Jean Baptiste Girardot's bluff-top trading post flourished here 250 years ago.

At Cape Girardeau, 125 miles south of St. Louis, the muddy-brown Mississippi runs southward with a current so strong you can easily follow it with your eye. From a perch atop Cape Rock Park, the bird's-eye view makes it plain why the river came to be called the Mighty Mississippi. The park provides the ideal setting for visitors to contemplate the many untold stories of the men and women who passed below in canoes, keelboats, gunboats and steamboats.

Cape Rock Park is built on the site of the original rock that jutted out into the river. This promontory once formed the only inland cape in the country. Although the rock was destroyed to make way for the railroad tracks visible below, the extraordinary view remains.

The winding river bends and turns, making its way through the green, forested, unspoiled banks that define the river. The landscape along the river begins to change here. The wooded bluffs and limestone cliffs of the Heartland give way to an ever-widening, swampy floodplain that wends its way south to the New Orleans delta.

Hub of the Region

The Spanish founded Cape Girardeau in 1792, but its name and character are a legacy of the French who once dominated the region. America acquired the frontier settlement in the Louisiana Purchase of 1803. Halfway between St. Louis and Memphis, Cape Girardeau thrived as a river port throughout the 1800s. Today, it's the region's biggest town and home to Southeast Missouri State University. With plenty of lodgings and restaurants, it's a good base for exploring the area.

A massive and colorful 20-foot-tall flood wall protects the city of 35,000 from the ravages of the river. Two murals decorate the wall, depicting people and events in the history of the city and state. Ten other murals are scattered around town. Two imposing floodgates access the river.

At the broad levee with a docking area, passengers disembark from the handful of riverboats that still

Cape Girardeau
descends to
the river.

chug upstream. Benches tempt visitors to linger a while and enjoy the calliope or Dixieland band music that often accompanies the bustle of a riverboat's arrival. As in days gone by, life seems a bit more exciting when a riverboat comes to town.

Historic homes and buildings in various stages of restoration survive throughout the city. For a commanding view of the Mississippi, head to the 1854 Common Pleas Courthouse. From a bluff overlooking the river, this building served as Union military headquarters and housed Confederate prisoners during the Civil War.

The nearby three-story structure on Water Street, now home to Port Cape Girardeau Restaurant, once served as the temporary headquarters for General Ulysses S. Grant when he commanded Union forces in southeastern Missouri and southern Illinois during the Civil War.

The Glenn House, a neoclassic-style Victorian home built in 1881, recalls the town's past glory. Like many historic homes in the region, it has an intricate front fence reminiscent of the famous ironwork found in New Orleans. Inside, elaborate stencils adorn the house's papered walls in the fashion of the day, and its rooms overflow with restored antique furniture, household items and period clothing. Trees and newer buildings slightly obscure the once magnificent panoramic river view.

All Aboard for Jackson

Make the short hop west to the town of Jackson, and you may spot a plume of thick, black smoke curling into the sky. Follow that smoke to find No. 5, a shiny, black 1946 steam locomotive operated by the St. Louis Iron Mountain & Southern Railway. Watch the hostler stoke the engine's firebox,

Steamboats still ply the big river.

CHET HANCHETT

Glenn House in Cape Girardeau recalls 19th-century prosperity.

a task that takes up to four hours before each run. Shovelful after shovelful of coal makes the steam that runs this old-fashioned train.

The hard-working engine pulls excursion and dinner trains through the quiet countryside. The train chugs along with American flags flying. It rolls past farms that already were old when the restored Pullman cars were new.

The ride isn't speedy—the railway has only 14 miles of track available. The trips are merely relaxing diversions. As the train huffs and puffs past country crossings, passengers wave enthusiastically to waiting cars that honk right back.

If you're feeling a bit more adventurous, choose an excursion that furnishes excitement. Experience the drama of days gone by, complete with a mock Jesse James and his gang on horseback holding up the train. Or join other passengers in solving a thrilling murder mystery over dinner.

A love of railroading keeps this old train on track, in top condition for the 100,000 passengers who ride each year. The engineer, fireman, brakeman and train chief volunteer countless hours maintaining the train

and the tracks. Their efforts preserve this shrieking, steam-belching, entertaining anachronism.

Take Your Camera To Burfordville

About 10 miles farther west is the bucolic community of Burfordville, where you'll find a picturesque, well-preserved piece of history. The Bollinger Mill State Historic Site, which has been used for milling since 1800, now has a restored four-story 1867 mill and a 140-foot-long covered bridge. Explore the hiking trails or linger long enough for a picnic lunch. Visitors glimpse the past by taking a guided tour that includes an interesting demonstration of water-powered millstones grinding fresh corn into meal.

The Old Mill Store sells local craft items, as well as soft drinks, ice cream and other refreshments. The grand stone-and-brick mill nestles next to a limestone dam that creates a small waterfall along the Whitewater River. In addition to the covered bridge, they form a remarkable setting that attracts artists and photographers from all over the country.

Planning Your Visit to Cape Girardeau and Jackson

For more information, contact: Cape Girardeau Convention & Visitors Bureau (800/777-0068) or (573/335-1631); Jackson Chamber of Commerce (573/243-8131).

LODGINGS

You'll find chain motels along I-55 (exit 96) on the outskirts of Cape Girardeau. Call ahead for accommodations at privately owned motels in Cape Girardeau and Jackson.

Bellevue Bed & Breakfast—Antique-filled rooms with private baths abound in a Queen Anne Victorian that flaunts "painted lady" colors in down-town Cape Girardeau. Doubles from $70 to $95 (800/768-6822).

Neumeyer's Bed & Breakfast—Three guest rooms with private baths provide seclusion in a newly remodeled Craftsman-style bungalow. A short walk beyond the wide veranda and thriving garden lies the Cape Girardeau riverfront. Doubles from $60 (573/335-0449).

Trisha's Bed & Breakfast—Four bedrooms, three with private baths, fill this restored 1905 Victorian home in Jackson just a few blocks from the train depot. You'll wake to a gourmet three-course breakfast. Doubles from $55 (800/651-0408 or 573/243-7427).

CAMPING

Trail of Tears State Park—Hiking trails and bluff-top river views surround picnic areas and wooded campsites (some with electrical hookups), located just 10 miles north of Cape Girardeau. The interpretive center tells about the Cherokees' forced march through this part of the Mississippi River Valley (573/334-1711).

DINING

Port Cape Girardeau Restaurant—Great barbecue is served in the historic 1830s riverfront building, along Water St. downtown. The site marks the former headquarters for General Ulysses S. Grant during the Civil War (573/334-0954).

Royal N'Orleans Club Restaurant—This elegant steak house at 300 Broadway offers Chateaubriand, hand-cut steaks, seafood and Creole house specials (573/335-8191).

My Daddy's Cheese-cake—Downtown on N. Main St., My Daddy's prepares more than 20 cheesecake varieties, including Mississippi Mud and the Gooey Louie cookie wedge (800/735-6765 or 573/335-6660).

Nicky's Whistle Stop Cafe—Known for authentic New Orleans-style cuisine, this diner and old-fashioned soda fountain occupies part of the train station along US-61 in Jackson. (573/243-0020).

SIGHTSEEING & MUSEUMS

Cape Rock Park—Found along E. Cape Rock Dr. north of town, this park provides excellent river views at the site of the original trading post that evolved into present-day Cape Girardeau.

The Glenn House—This historic house museum along S. Spanish St. exemplifies the Victorian elegance associated with prosperous homeowners in the 1900s. The house is open Saturdays and Sundays, April through December (573/334-1177).

Old St. Vincent's Church—At Main St. and William St., this antebellum Gothic church exhibits more than 100 medieval-design plaster masks (573/335-6427).

Rose Display Garden—

The garden in Capaha Park holds more than 40 beds with approximately 185 varieties. **Fort D**—This last remaining fort of four built during the Civil War to protect the town from assault by either land or water is now maintained as a city park and located in the southern part of Cape Girardeau. **St. Louis Iron Mountain and Southern Railway**— A 1946 steam engine pulls vintage train cars

Methodist Chapel is the oldest Protestant church structure west of the Mississippi. Look for the church off US-61 north of Cape Girardeau (800/777-0068 or 573/243-2774). **Bollinger Mill State Historic Site**—The picturesque setting includes a working grist mill, a gift shop, picnic sites, hiking trails and one of the few remaining covered bridges in the state (573/243-4591).

museum showcases Native American Mississippian artifacts, art and military items, as well as temporary exhibits of regional history and artwork (573/651-2260).

SHOPPING

Downtown Cape Girardeau's elite shops include: **Parson's Stained Glass**, a gallery with hand-fashioned stained glass, including lamps, kaleidoscopes, "sun-catchers" and made-to-order pieces (573/334-0960); **Judith Anne's**, a Victorian gift shop selling candles and other collectibles (573/339-1766); and **Chrisman's Outfitters**, specializing in fly-fishing equipment and artwork (573/335-3311). **Antiques Guide**—You'll find a variety of crafts and antiques shops throughout the area. For a complete listing of more than 70 dealers and a map of locations, call Cape Girardeau Convention & Visitors Bureau (800/777-0068 or 573/335-1631). **Gallery 100**—This downtown showcase for area artists is operated by the Southeast Missouri Council of the Arts (573/334-9233). **Esicar's Old Hickory Smokehouse**—Along US-61, this local favorite sells old-fashioned sugar-cured,

FRANK OBERLE

Climb aboard the St. Louis Iron Mountain & Southern Railway near Jackson for leisurely trips.

while special excursions feature dinner, music, murder mysteries or other entertainment (800/455-7245). **Oliver House**—The carefully restored 1854 home along E. Adams St. in Jackson once was the residence of the woman who designed the Missouri state flag. (573-243-2560). **Old McKendree Chapel**—The 1819

Cape River Heritage Museum—Housed in an old fire station, this museum displays Mississippi River-related artifacts and items from the town's history such as the Missouri state flag, which was made in the town (573/334-0405). **University Museum**— Located in Memorial Hall on the Southeast Missouri State University campus, the

hickory-smoked hams, bacon and sausage (573/335-9283).

FESTIVALS

Riverfest—Hosting crafts booths and musical performances, Riverfest occurs in mid-June in historic downtown Cape Girardeau along the riverfront (800/777-0068).

STATE PARK

Trail of Tears State Park—Along State-177, sharp ridges, steep ravines and limestone bluffs towering more than 175 feet above the river characterize these 3,400 acres of natural forest. The only state park bordering the Mississippi, it commemorates the exile and forced march of 13,000 Cherokees. The tragic incident resulted in the deaths of up to one-fourth of the Native Americans during the trek. This is the site where the group camped after crossing the river by ferry during the winter of 1838–39.

The countryside remains much as it was when the Cherokees journeyed here. Follow the hiking trails to overlook with river views. There are a small lake for fishing and boating, and a camping area within sight of the river. An interpretive center documents the Native Americans' forced relocation through paintings, maps, memorabilia and personal testimonies.

Tower Rock Natural Area—South of town, you can see one of the few remaining natural landmarks along the river. Tower Rock is 60 feet tall and 100 yards at the base. It was first identified by explorers Joliet and Marquette in 1673, and President Ulysses S. Grant ordered it preserved in 1871 when engineers cleared the channel. This solitary rock

Overlooking the Mississippi River from Trail of Tears Park, located 10 miles north of Cape Girardeau.

stands majestically in the Mississippi River and has been noted by travelers along the river for centuries.

OTHER PLACES TO VISIT IN THE AREA

Commerce

Tiny Commerce sits just a few miles south of Cape Girardeau. Established in 1790, it was once a bustling river town. It sits on the river banks and boasts the "best view of the river between St. Louis and Memphis," according to locals. There are no river bluffs, swampy areas or levee walls separating the town from the river, so you can walk right down to the banks to fish or watch the Mississippi roll on by.

The Anderson Guest House, built in 1847, is a spotlessly clean bed and breakfast housed in a restored home perched high above the river. Two simply furnished guest rooms provide views of the Mississippi River that reveal a natural shoreline free of buildings or industry. There's an elegant parlor with Victorian-style antiques and reproductions, plus a modern kitchen where owner Susan Steel provides a full-course breakfast.

River Ridge Winery, nestled on gently rolling slopes less than 2 miles north of town, features a well-stocked gift shop and promises plenty of personal attention from the winemaker and his wife, Jerry and Joannie Smith (573/264-3712). This family-run operation, in business since 1994, produces 1,500 gallons of wine each year.

The couple's modest four-room farmhouse, built in 1894, sits right off the leafy two-lane road, County-321, and serves as a tasting center and gift shop. A 200-year-old catalpa tree shades the gingerbread-trimmed house, which sports wooden porch posts with actual wine bottles built into them.

The vineyard covers more than 4 acres. The winery makes Continental-style wines from grapes similar to those grown in California and France. Eight varieties of dry and semidry wine are offered for sale and tasting.

The gift shop stocks dinnerware, baskets, wine accoutrements, Christmas ornaments and gourmet food from all over the world.

Picnic tables and chairs scattered over the property invite visitors to sit a spell and enjoy the wine and the view. You can buy a picnic basket for two and walk to the vineyards or hike to the river. If you want to talk wine, this is the place to go.

LODGINGS

The Anderson Guest House—Two spotlessly clean guest rooms are available in this historic home on a bluff over-looking the river along Water St. Doubles from $80 (800/705-1317 or 573/264-4123).

SIGHTSEEING AND MUSEUMS

Commerce Museum— Numerous artifacts and photographs donated by local residents are housed in this old church (573/264-3960). For information about Commerce, call: 573/264-2199.

Other Towns

Charming tiny towns and historic natural areas surround Cape Girardeau, providing the perfect retreat for a leisurely drive in the country. US-61 winds around through rural countryside to reveal rustic Old Appleton. This tiny village of 80 people provides a pretty-as-a-picture site on the banks of Apple

Creek, with a reconstructed bridge that dates to 1879. Stop at the Apple Creek Pottery, where you'll discover hand-thrown stoneware pottery, antiques and collectibles (573/788-2110). Take Hwy.-A out of town toward the river and the early German settlements of Frohna, Wittenberg and Altenburg, settled in 1839 by immigrants from Saxony seeking religious freedom in the New World. At the Saxon Lutheran Memorial site in Frohna, you can see a number of vintage log cabins, along with barns and outbuildings. At the visitors center and museum, displays relate more about the original German settlers (573/824-5404). Altenberg is the site of Concordia Log College and Seminary, the first Lutheran seminary west of the Mississippi, established in 1839 (573/824-5221). For a taste of the Old Country, stop by Tric's Restaurant along Hwy.-C in Altenburg. Plate lunches and buffets feature German-style home cooking (573/824-5387). For more area information, call the Altenberg Bank (573/824-5221).

By Jane Cosby

SOUTHERN MISSOURI AND ILLINOIS

There's a hint of Dixie where the Mississippi River leaves the Heartland.

Although the map says you're in the Midwest, the southernmost parts of Missouri and Illinois along the Mississippi River seem part of the rural South. Agricultural and sparsely populated, they're also friendly, relaxed and thoroughly homespun. Most of the area's residents speak with a soft twang; a few have a more pronounced accent reminiscent of the region where the Mississippi empties into the Gulf of Mexico.

A Rich and Varied Land

The Mississippi grows broader, deeper and muddier as it receives the Ohio River about 150 miles southeast of St. Louis. The river valley here teems with birds and wildlife. Red-winged blackbirds flash past frequently, and herons trail their long, ungainly legs as they flap between wetlands. This is part of the Mississippi flyway, a 14-state path used by migratory waterfowl. During the winter months, countless geese and ducks, as well as American bald eagles, flock to the area.

Flat farmscapes divide neatly into mile-square fields, shaded here and there by massive live oaks and edged with wildflowers. Enormous pieces of farm equipment seem to hulk in fields—many of them unidentifiable to city folks. Occasionally tractors crawl the back highways, slowing traffic.

Take a walk in Big Oak Tree State Park, and you'll discover what the first settlers in this area encountered: a thick canopy of trees that completely shades the woodland paths. This remote, day-use-only park includes a modest interpretive center and a boardwalk that provides access to the park's swampy wooded terrain. Big Oak Tree encompasses one of the few remaining virgin bottomland forests and cypress swamps in the country.

Southwestern Illinois' history is as rich as its soil. Mound-building Indians known as the Mississippians lived here between 1000 and 1400 A.D. Their mounds, located in low hills that dot the landscape, serve as ancient reminders of these

FRANK OBERLE

Huge cypresses abound in southern Illinois.

people. Weary armies waged bloody Civil War battles here, fighting for access to the Mississippi River. But the single most dramatic event in this region's recorded history took place in New Madrid, Missouri.

New Madrid

The tranquil farmland surrounding the small town of New Madrid (population: 3,350) belies the turmoil below the surface. This is the epicenter of the New Madrid Seismic Zone, a complex of earthquake faults 150 miles long and 50 miles wide that covers five states. In 1811, the strongest earthquakes ever recorded in North America struck the town founded to be the capital of Spain's holdings in the New World. The nightmare began in mid-December. The earth convulsed for eight weeks. Gaping crevasses swallowed farmhouses, shifting terrain uprooted massive trees, landslides obliterated familiar landmarks, and terrified settlers fled.

Today, in the quiet and intimate New Madrid Historical Museum downtown, you can see scientific explanations and firsthand accounts of the quakes that struck with awesome power. For a time, they caused the Mississippi River to run backward and church bells to clang in far-off Boston.

An observation deck across the street from the museum offers a panoramic view of the bend marking one of the widest points on the river. New Madrid also was the site of an important Civil War battle along the Mississippi River, which meanders past the town beyond a soaring levee.

One of the grandest mansions in the region, the Hunter-Dawson Home State Historic Site, rises on the north edge of New Madrid. Tour the 15-room antebellum showplace built of yellow cypress in 1858 by a prosperous local merchant. Elaborately costumed guides answer questions and demonstrate the southern charm characteristic of 19th-century gentry.

Cairo

Drive over the river and into Illinois. Corn and cotton flourish in long stretches of rich bottomland fields. Dead trees stand bereft of limbs and

The lodge at Illinois' Giant City State Park.

FRANK OBERLE

New Madrid's 1858 Hunter Dawson home.

FRANK OBERLE

leaves, grim reminders of flood waters that rose then fell, leaving destruction in their wake.

Cairo (population: 4,800) sits where the blue waters of the Ohio River meet the Mississippi's muddy flow. Early settlers compared this fertile river land to the Nile River delta in Egypt and named the town accordingly. (Residents pronounce it KAY-roh.) Cairo was a vital Union outpost during the Civil War, but that period of history is only a shadow today.

On to the South

On the town's southern edge is Fort Defiance State Park, an ever-narrowing spit of land that ends where the rivers meet. The two powerful currents collide, forming a seam extending outward across the glinting surface as far as you can see. A three-story lookout tower provides an imposing view of the confluence.

South of the Ohio River, as you enter Kentucky, the Mississippi begins to narrow. Much of the land around the river is reserved as wildlife and waterfowl refuges. The Dorena-Hickman Ferry connects the two towns for which it's named. For a small toll, the ferry transports vehicles from Dorena, Missouri, to Hickman, Kentucky. The fabulous only-on-the-water view of the river is well worth the fare.

The New Madrid earthquakes of 1811-12 reconfigured the landscape here. During the quakes, a large area of land sank. Later, water filled the impression, forming Reelfoot Lake, Tennessee's only natural lake. This fishing resort area, located in upper northwestern Tennessee, has an inn and restaurant on the lake's north side with history and wildlife exhibits on the south.

A boardwalk outside the visitors center winds through a grove of partially submerged bald cypresses, allowing visitors to study these unusual trees that push their root system up through the water. The roots, which look like wooden stalagmites scattered throughout the swamp, feed oxygen to the trees. The cypresses, as well as other submerged vegetation, create a natural fish hatchery that draws anglers. In summer, you can take a pontoon boat cruise. Cold weather brings hundreds of bald eagles to the area, along with eager bird-watchers.

Planning Your Visit to Southern Missouri and Illinois, Kentucky/ Tennessee

For information contact: Missouri Tourist Information Center, New Madrid (573/643-2654); Illinois Travel Information Center (800/2CONNECT); Southernmost Illinois Tourism Bureau (800/248-4373); Kentucky Dept. of Parks (800/255-PARK); Tennessee Dept. of Environment and Conservation (888/TN-PARKS).

LODGINGS

You'll find chain motels on the outskirts of Sikeston, Missouri, Paducah, Kentucky, and Marion and Carbondale, Illinois. Check ahead with tourist information agencies for other accommodations.

Airpark Inn—Along Reelfoot Lake in Tennessee, the inn has 20 units near towering cypress trees. Doubles from $56, suites from $75 (800/250-8617).

Cypress Point Resort—This Reelfoot Lake area resort offers 24 units. Doubles from $45 (901/253-6654).

CAMPING

Reelfoot Lake State Park—This 18,000-acre natural lake located along Rte. 1 in Tiptonville, Tennessee, is rich in submerged forests and acres of water lilies, making it an ideal spot for anglers and nature lovers. A visitors center provides exhibits about the origin of the lake, as well as its complex ecosystem. There are more than 100 sites at two campgrounds (901/253-7756).

Columbus-Belmont State Park—A 156-acre Kentucky state park preserves the site of a major Civil War battle. Original trenches dug by Confederate forces along the bluffs still exist *(see Other Places to Visit on page 140)*. The park's 38 camping sites are equipped with electrical and water hookups (502/677-2327).

DINING

Lambert's Cafe—Located off I-55 about one block from the factory outlet mall in Sikeston, Missouri, this family-style restaurant emphasizes fun. It's the home of "throwed rolls" (for laughs, workers toss warm rolls to diners) and hearty, delicious "pass arounds," all-you-can-eat side dishes (573/471-4261).

Rosie's Colonial Restaurant and Tavern—For more than 50 years, this establishment along State-61 in New Madrid, Missouri, has served home-style dishes, such as chicken fried steak, catfish and shrimp (573/748-7665).

SIGHTSEEING

Major highways criss-cross the region, linking main communities such as Sikeston, Missouri, Paducah, Kentucky, and Carbondale and Marion, Illinois. Secondary roads lead to most attractions in this sparsely populated area. State-3, part of the Great River Road, parallels the Mississippi River in southwest Illinois. US-77, running parallel to I-55, follows the river's Missouri bank. US-51 in Kentucky and State-78 in Tennessee are the roads closest to the river. They wind through hills and valleys, only occasionally providing a glimpse of the river.

Big Oak Tree State Park—Primarily a swamp forest of towering trees, the park resembles the natural conditions of this area before settlers pushed west. Quietly stroll a boardwalk through wetlands to observe virgin forest and various wildlife, including colorful woodpeckers and flying squirrels. Big Oak Tree State Park is located southeast of East Prairie, Missouri, off State-102 (573/649-3149).

Towosahgy State Historic Site—This 64-acre site preserves the location of a once-fortified Mississippian Indian village. Of the seven mounds visible here, the largest one is 16 feet tall. Drive southeast of East Prairie, Missouri, off State-77 on County-FF (573/649-3149).

Hunter-Dawson Home State Historic Site—The 15-room residence typifies the splendid mansions that once

Northwest of Cairo, Illinois, Horseshoe Lake, reminiscent of the Deep South, resembles a southern bayou.

lined the river banks and housed successful Missouri Bootheel gentry in New Madrid. (573/748-5340).

Mound City National Cemetery—More than 2,700 markers honor Union and Confederate dead who are buried in this parklike cemetery at Mound City 5 miles north of Cairo, Illinois. One gravestone simply reads, "Confederate spy." Verses from the poignant poem "Bivouac of the Dead" border the cemetery walkway.

Fort Defiance State Park—This small point of land is located 2 miles south of Cairo, Illinois. A magnificent vantage point, it marks the meeting of the Ohio and Mississippi rivers. The lookout tower and picnic tables make the park worth a stop.

Casino Aztar—This noncruising gambling boat anchors in downtown Caruthersville, Missouri. The waiting area includes a sports bar and restaurant (573/333-6000).

MUSEUMS

Cairo Custom House—The 1872 customs house once housed a federal court and post office. The ground floor displays a desk used by General Ulysses S. Grant and other period articles (618/734-1019 or 613/734-2932).

Magnolia Manor—Italianate styling characterizes this five-

story, 14-room mansion containing a bed in which Ulysses S. Grant slept (618/734-0201).

Safford Memorial Library—History buffs will be interested in this working library in Cairo. A collection of Civil War documents, antiques and paintings of the era are on display (618/734-1840).

New Madrid Historical Museum—A variety of displays at One Main St. depict the great earthquake, prehistoric Indians, explorers and riverboat trade that characterized this small Missouri town (573/748-5944).

OUTDOOR RECREATION

Horseshoe Lake Conservation Area—Featuring large stands of tupelo, swamp cottonwood and cypress trees located northwest of Cairo, Illinois, this area is reminiscent of the Deep South. It's especially noteworthy for bald eagle sightings during the fall and winter (618/776-5689).

Union County Conservation Area—Numerous shallow sloughs and other water areas dominate more than 6,000 acres located off State-3 west of Jonesboro, Illinois. The area is a natural stopping-off point for 50,000 Canadian geese during winter. Avid birders will appreciate the experience, despite the cold weather (618/833-5175).

SHOPPING

River Birch Antique Gallery—Dealers in Sikeston, Missouri, sell interesting collectibles and antiques (573/472-4700). Sikeston Factory Outlet Stores—For a day or more of shopping, browse through more than 30 stores at the junction of I-55 and US-62 in Sikeston, Missouri (800/908-SHOP).

Ohio rivers in southern Illinois, reveals scenic treasures at every turn. Beyond Carbondale, Marion and Harrisburg, the Ozark Mountains rise in a high range of rounded, green hills. Extending between the rivers, they form the rugged spine of 270,000-acre Shawnee National Forest.

Twisting, often unmarked roads link campgrounds, trailheads and quiet little towns with colorful names such as Muddy, Ozark and Lick Creek. Here, relentless summer sun and moist air fade crimson paint on out-

barges glide past villages that celebrated centennials decades before the Civil War.

The jobless Illinois men who flocked to the Civilian Conservation Corps during the 1930s expertly crafted Giant City Lodge, the expansive centerpiece of 4,000-acre Giant City State Park about 10 miles south of Carbondale. Many guests take time to admire the sandstone and white-oak structure's cathedral ceiling of massive logs, the giant stone fireplace and rugged handmade

Large Rock formations overlook the forest in the Garden of the Gods area of the Shawnee National Forest located by the Mississippi and Ohio rivers.

OTHER PLACES TO VISIT IN THE AREA
Shawnee National Forest

With its mysterious cypress swamps, rocky canyons, trees and rolling Ozark Mountains, the Shawnee National Forest region, bounded by the Mississippi and

buildings to chalky pink and rust corrugated tin roofs in streaks of orange.

Some lanes lead to broad sloughs, eerie and silent under towering cypresses that extend knobby "knees" upward from the algae-carpeted water. Along the Mississippi and Ohio,

oak-and-leather furnishings. The aromas of fried chicken and side dishes entice visitors to the dining room for family-style feasts. The lodge, park and generous dinners number among the national forest's best-known attractions. At Garden of the Gods, a

55-mile drive east of Giant City Lodge, hikers and sightseers perch atop sandstone palisades and huge rock "toadstools" that rise above the forest. About 10 miles northwest of the lodge, a steep path leads to Pomona Natural Bridge. In a cool, shady valley, the 30-foot-high sandstone arch, dappled with moss, spans a quiet, gravel-bottomed brook that steadily carved this wonder for eons. Although rarely visited and largely overlooked, this amazing part of Illinois offers visitors an uncommon experience.

LODGINGS

Motel rooms are available in Carbondale and Marion. In addition, you'll find a few inns and bed and breakfasts in the villages along the rivers and near the national forest. Giant City Lodge— At this centerpiece of Giant City State Park, guests can choose from 34 cabins. Popular fried chicken dinners are served in the lodge's restaurant. Doubles from $49 to $90 (618/457-4921). The Goddard Place Bed & Breakfast—Discover a peaceful retreat with three private guest rooms on 70 acres, plus a large stocked fishing pond, in Anna, Illinois.

Doubles from $55 (618/833-6256 or 618/833-8311).

DINING

Elizabethtown Fish and Marine—This floating marina and restaurant in Elizabethtown, 40 miles southeast of Marion, specializes in Ohio River catfish dinners (618/287-2333).

SIGHTSEEING

The best guides for getting around are detailed, large-scale Shawnee National Forest maps you can pick up at national forest offices in Elizabethtown, Harrisburg, Jonesboro, Murphysboro and Vienna. The maps detail the entire region.

CAMPING

Shawnee National Forest—More than 450 campsites at 16 designated campgrounds range from primitive dispersed (make-your-own) campsites to developed campground areas with beaches, showers and electricity (800/699-6637).

For area information, contact: Harrisburg Chamber of Commerce (888/844-8687).

Northwest Kentucky

Traveling across the Ohio River and into Kentucky over a winding, shady highway, you'll drive through small towns

that became isolated when bypassed by the interstates. Old buildings, some shabby, others tidy and lovingly cared for, are interspersed among the trees and brush along the rural highway. Wickliffe, originally home to a group of ancient Mississippian Indians, is typical of towns in this region. The Wickliffe Mounds Research Center preserves a Mississippian Indian ceremonial site and trade center that include several mounds. An interpretive visitors center about these Native Americans is open from March through November (502/335-3681).

Farther south in the town of Columbus, Columbus-Belmont State Park preserves fields of battle. Across the river in Missouri, Ulysses S. Grant attacked Confederate forces in his first major fight of the war. From Kentucky river bluffs, 140 Confederate cannons bombarded Union forces arrayed on the western bank of the river. A 2½-mile trail guides visitors around the site. A small, white frame building, once a hospital during the battle, now provides narratives and a pictorial map of the engagement (502/677-2327).

By Randy Cosby

The Stagecoach Trail begins in Galena, Illinois, page 61.

Lake City Marina on Lake Pepin in Wisconsin, page 24.

Midwest Living® Books
An imprint of Meredith® Books

Mississippi River Getaways
Project Editor: Judith P. Knuth
Art Director: Angie Hoogensen
Copy Chief: Catherine Hamrick
Copy and Production Editor:
    Terri Fredrickson
Contributing Copy Editor:
    Angela K. Renkoski
Contributing Researchers:
    Joan Luckett, Nancy Singh
Contributing Proofreader:
    Deb Morris Smith
Map Illustrator: Mike Burns
Electronic Production Coordinator:
    Paula Forest
Editorial and Design Assistants:
    Judy Bailey, Kaye Chabot,
    Karen Schirm
Production Director:
    Douglas M. Johnston
Production Manager: Pam Kvitne
Assistant Prepress Manager:
    Marjorie J. Schenkelberg

Meredith® Books
Editor in Chief: James D. Blume
Design Director: Matt Strelecki
Managing Editor: Gregory H. Kayko

Director, Sales & Marketing, Retail:
    Michael A. Peterson
Director, Sales & Marketing, Special
    Markets: Rita McMullen
Director, Sales & Marketing, Home &
    Garden Center Channel: Ray Wolf
Director, Operations: George A. Susral

Vice President, General Manager:
    Jamie L. Martin

Midwest Living® **Magazine**
Editor: Dan Kaercher
Managing Editor: Barbara Humeston

Meredith Publishing Group
President, Publishing Group:
    Christopher M. Little
Vice President, Consumer Marketing
    & Development: Hal Oringer

Meredith Corporation
Chairman and Chief Executive
    Officer: William T. Kerr

Chairman of the Executive
    Committee: E. T. Meredith III

All of us at Meredith® Books are
dedicated to providing you with the
information and ideas you need. We
welcome your comments and
suggestions. Write to us at: Meredith®
Books, Travel Department, 1716 Locust
St., Des Moines, IA 50309-3023.

If you would like to order additional
copies of any of our books, check with
your local bookstore.